P9-BEE-458

NTC's
SPANISH
GRAMMAR

Author
Rosa María Martín

Consultant
Tim Connell

NTC Publishing Group
NTC/Contemporary Publishing Company

Library of Congress Cataloging-in-Publication Data

Martín, Rosa María.
　　　NTC's Spanish grammar / Rosa María Martín.
　　　　　　p.　　cm. — (NTC's grammar series)
　　　English and Spanish
　　　Includes index.
　　　　ISBN 0-8092-7225-6
　　　　1. Spanish language—Grammar—Handbooks, manuals, etc.
　　I. Title.　　II. Series
　　PC4112.M274　　1997
　　468.2'421—dc21　　　　　　　　　　　　　　　97-36713
　　　　　　　　　　　　　　　　　　　　　　　　　　CIP

Also available:
　　NTC's French Grammar
　　NTC's Italian Grammar
　　NTC's German Grammar

Cover artwork by Elaine Cox
Published in cooperation with BBC Enterprises Limited

This edition first published in 1998 by NTC Publishing Group
An imprint of NTC/Contemporary Publishing Company
4255 West Touhy Avenue
Lincolnwood (Chicago), Illinois 60646-1975 U.S.A.
Copyright © 1995, 1998 by Rosa María Martín
All rights reserved. No part of this book may be reproduced, stored in a
retrieval system, or transmitted in any form or by any means, electronic,
mechanical, photocopying, recording, or otherwise, without the prior
permission of NTC/Contemporary Publishing Company.
Printed in the United States of America
International Standard Book Number: 0-8442-7225-6

15　　14　　13　　12　　11　　10　　9　　8　　7　　6　　5　　4　　3　　2　　1

■ Introduction

NTC's *Spanish Grammar* is for adult learners, whether
learning at home or in adult/continuing education or
nonspecialist college language courses. It is also ideal for
high school students.

It is a practical reference book that makes Spanish
grammar accessible to English-speaking learners, and it is
the ideal complement to any course book. The emphasis is
on clear and concise explanation of the core structures of
Spanish, illustrated by examples using current, everyday
language.

It is not necessary to have a detailed formal knowledge of
English grammar to use this book since the use of
technical grammatical terms has been restricted to those
that are essential. There is also a glossary to help clarify
these terms.

The book is designed to allow easy and rapid consultation.
It comprises:

- a list of contents—a quick way to find the section or
  subsection you want

- a glossary of grammatical terms

- grammar explanations clearly laid out in numbered
  sections and subsections. The first half of the book
  covers nouns, articles, adjectives, pronouns, adverbs,
  and prepositions. The second half focuses on verbs:
  formation, use, and irregular forms.

- verb tables—the patterns for regular verbs and for
  commonly used irregular verbs

- a fully comprehensive, easy-to-use index, which lists
  key words in Spanish and English as well as
  grammatical terms.

■ Contents

Adjective

An adjective is a word that describes a noun. For example:

*It is a **big** house.*   *The windows are **big**.*

Adverb

An adverb is a word that adds information about the verb or about another adverb or adjective. For example:

*She read the text **carefully**.* [manner]

*Please wait **here**.* [place]

*The exam is **tomorrow**.* [time]

*The exam was **very** difficult.* [degree]

*Do you come here **often**?* [frequency]

Article

In English, *a* and *an* are the **indefinite articles**, and *the* is the **definite article**.

Conditional

A conditional sentence contains a clause beginning with *if*, *unless*, etc., that states what must happen before the action of the other clause can be done. For example:

***If it rains**, we will have to go home.*

*You can't attend university **unless you pass your exams**.*

Conjunction

A conjunction is a word that makes a connection between words, phrases, or clauses. For example:

*My present was small **but** nice.*

Gender

Gender shows whether a word is masculine or feminine.

Infinitive

The infinitive form of the verb is the base form and the form that usually appears in dictionaries. In English, the infinitive is often used with *to*, e.g., *I'd like **to go***.

Interjection

An interjection is a word that shows an emotional state or attitude. For example:

Hey! Come back here.   *Oh! That's terrible news.*

Interrogative

An interrogative sentence has the form of a question. For example:

Did you open the window?

Modal

Modal verbs are used with another verb to distinguish between possibility and actuality. For example:

*I **may** be late tonight.* [possibility]
*They **can** play outside.* [permission]

Mood

The mood of a verb can reveal a particular attitude to what is said or written or toward the person being addressed. For example, in English you use the **indicative mood** to state or question what you consider to be facts:

*She **sat** down.*   ***Are** you **coming**?*

You use the **imperative mood** when you are telling or ordering someone to do something:

***Be** quiet!*   ***Put** it on the table.*

You might use the **subjunctive mood** when you want to express wishes, possibilities, or doubts:

*It is essential that you **be** there.*
*If I **were** you, I'd do it.*

Negative

A word, phrase, or sentence that denies something is negative. In English, the most common way of showing this is with *not*. For example:

*I am **not** very happy!*

Noun

A noun refers to a person, a thing, or an abstract idea such as a feeling or quality. For example:

*The **woman** drove off.*   *The **children** patted the **dog**.*

Number

Number shows the difference between **singular** and **plural**. For example:

*The green **box is** empty.* [singular]
*The green **boxes are** empty.* [plural]

Object

Many verbs are used with objects. Objects are usually nouns or pronouns. The object is the noun or pronoun that is affected by the verb. For example:

*I asked **a question**.* [direct object]
*I asked **him**.* [indirect object]

Participle

A participle is a form of the verb that can be used with other verbs or sometimes as an adjective or a noun. For example:

*I like **walking** to work.* [present participle]
*She has **broken** her arm.* [past participle]

Person

Person is the system that shows the number of the people talking or writing. For example:

I [first person singular]   *it* [third person singular]
you [second person singular]   *we* [first person plural]
he [third person singular]   *you* [second person plural]
she [third person singular]   *they* [third person plural]

Possessive

A possessive is a word that shows ownership or possession. For example:

my, your, his, her, its, our, your, their [possessive adjectives]

mine, yours, his, hers, ours, yours, theirs [possessive pronouns]
*the **student's** books/the **students'** books* [possessive nouns]

Preposition

A preposition is a word that is used before a noun or a pronoun, and that shows the relationship between that noun or pronoun and the rest of the sentence. For example:

*I went **to** the library.*   *Put it **in** the cupboard.*

Pronoun

A pronoun is a word that is used instead of a noun or a noun phrase in a sentence. For example:

*Where is Elspeth? **She** left the meeting early.*
*I gave **him** the money.*

Subject

The subject of a sentence is the word or phrase that represents the person or thing carrying out the action of the verb. For example:

***The student** is learning Italian.*
***The students** are learning Italian.*

Tense

The form of a verb shows whether you are referring to the past, the present, or the future. This system of forms is called the tense system. For example:

*The student **works** hard.* [present tense verb]
*The student **worked** hard.* [past tense verb]

Verb

A verb usually refers to an action or state. For example:

*The children **patted** the dog.*
*The green box **is** empty.*

2 Pronunciation and Spelling

2.1 The Spanish Alphabet

The Spanish alphabet consists of 27 letters. Here they are with their names:

a	a	h	hache	ñ	eñe	u	u
b	be	i	i	o	o	v	uve
c	ce	j	jota	p	pe	w	uve doble
d	de	k	ka	q	cu	x	equis
e	e	l	ele	r	erre	y	i griega
f	efe	m	eme	s	ese	z	zeta
g	ge	n	ene	t	te		

Until recently there were two more letters in the alphabet: **ch** and **ll**. These have now disappeared as separate letters by order of the Spanish Royal Academy and have become combined letters as in English and other European languages: **ch** = **c** + **h** and **ll** = **l** + **l**.

However, they can still to be found in dictionaries and books as one letter: **ch (che)**, **ll (elle)**.

■ **2.1.1** Letters of the alphabet are feminine: la **a**, la **be**, la **hache**.

2.2 Pronunciation and Spelling

Spanish is a language where most words are written as they are pronounced, with very few exceptions; there is not much difference between spelling and pronunciation.

■ **2.2.1** Vowels

Spanish has five vowels: a, e, i, o, u. They are short and clear and each one always has the same sound. Unlike English they are always pronounced.

■ 2.2.2 Consonants

In Spanish in general one sound corresponds to one letter and pronunciation of consonants does not pose many problems. The following rules of pronunciation are to be considered as specific to the Spanish language and might cause problems:

- b and v

  Both sound the same in Spanish and they are both pronounced like the English b, as in *big*. In the middle of a word it has a slightly softer sound:

b, v = b	beber	vacaciones	*big*
	cabeza	cerveza	

- c and z

c + e, i = [th]	centro, cine	*theater*
c + a, o, u = [k]	casa, coche, cuanto	*koala*
z + a, o, u = [th]	zapato, cerveza	*thorough*

  Note that in Latin America and in parts of the south of Spain ce, ci, and z are pronounced like s: cine sounds like sine; vez sounds like ves.

- h

  h is always silent in pronunciation but it must be written:
  hablar   helado   hielo   ¡hola!

- k and q

  k is only found in foreign words: kilómetro
  The sound [k] before e and i is obtained with qu. q is always written followed by u:
  qu + e, i = [k]   queso, quinientos   *kilogram*

  Note c + u (not q + u) the u is pronounced: ¿Cuánto cuesta?

  But: Quiero queso (the u is not pronounced).

- j and g

  j is pronounced at the back of the throat, rather like the ch in Scottish *loch* as in: jamón   joven

  g is pronounced in the same way as j before e and i: general   ginebra

  Both ge, gi and je, ji are pronounced the same and can be easily confused when writing. But note that there are a lot more words written in Spanish with ge, gi than with je, ji.

  g + a, o, u sounds as in the English *go, good*: Galicia   gorra   guapo

  gue, gui sound like the g in *get* in English. The u between the g and e or i is never pronounced: guerra   guitarra

  However there are some words in Spanish with the sound combinations [gwe] and [gwi], although not very common. They are written as güe, güi; the u must have a diaeresis: ü (this is the only use of diaeresis in Spanish): nicaragüense   lingüista

- ñ

  ñ is pronounced as in ny in *canyon*: mañana

- r

  r is pronounced differently according to where it appears in the word. At the beginning of a word and after l, n, or s the r is strong and it is rolled like a Scottish r: rosa   rojo   alrededor   sonreír   Israel

  To obtain the same sound between vowels we have to write rr: perro   carro

  If there is only one r between vowels the sound is softer and more similar to the English r in *cereal*: pero   caro

• **s**

  In parts of southern Spain and Latin America an **s** placed at the end of a word is not pronounced. The plural and singular may therefore be confused in pronunciation: **las casas** sounds like **[la casa]**.

2.3 Stress

In Spanish only one syllable in each word is stressed. The stress is free, which means it can be on any syllable. To establish which syllable of the word is stressed there are simple rules to follow:

■ **2.3.1** With words ending in a vowel or a combination of vowels or with the consonant **-n** or **-s**, the stress goes on the penultimate syllable: **ca**sa   **co**sas   **co**men

■ **2.3.2** With words ending in a consonant other than **-n** or **-s**, the stress goes on the last syllable: co**mer**   sa**lud**

■ **2.3.3** Words of one syllable only are always written without an accent: pie   diez   ya

2.4 Accents

■ **2.4.1** An accent is needed if the stress falls on the last syllable of a word ending in a vowel or **-n** or **-s**:
  salí   compraré   camión   salís

■ **2.4.2** An accent is needed if the stress falls on the penultimate syllable in a word ending in a consonant, except for **-n** or **-s**: cárcel   difícil   Martínez

■ **2.4.3** If the stress falls on the antepenultimate (third last) syllable it always has an accent:
  bolígrafo   régimen   física

■ **2.4.4** As mentioned above, words of one syllable are always written without an accent except when two words are homonyms. These are words that have the same form but a different meaning and that are often distinguished by the accent:

de	*of*	dé	subjunctive form of **dar**
el	*the*	él	*he*
mi	*my*	mí	*me* (after preposition)
si	*if*	sí	*yes*

2.5 Capital Letters

Spanish uses capital letters less frequently than English. They are used at the beginning of a sentence and after a period:

Ana llegó a casa. Entró.   *Ana arrived home. She went in.*

■ **2.5.1** Capital letters are not used for:

a months, seasons, and days of the week:
   septiembre   domingo

b languages, peoples, or adjectives of nationality:
   Hablo **español.**   *I speak Spanish.*
   Soy **alemán.**   *I am German.*

2.6 Question and Exclamation Mark

There are two signs for a question mark: ¿ placed at the beginning of the sentence and ? placed at the end. The same occurs with the exclamation mark: ¡ at the beginning and ! at the end:

   ¿Quieres ir al cine   *Would you like to go to the*
   conmigo esta tarde?   *movies with me this afternoon?*
   ¡Qué calor!   *What a heat!*

3 Nouns

Nouns are words used to name people, animals, and things. They are words such as *child*, *cat*, *table*. In Spanish they vary in gender and in number: **niño, niña** (*child*), **niños, niñas** (*children*), **mesa** (*table*), **mesas** (*tables*).

In Spanish all nouns are masculine or feminine whether they refer to people, animals, or things.

There is a natural gender, referring to males and females, and a grammatical gender, which is applied to all things.

3.1 Gender Endings

■ **3.1.1** Masculine nouns referring to people, animals, or things usually end in -o:

  un chico *a boy*   **el** perro *the dog*   **el** vaso *the glass*

■ **3.1.2** Feminine nouns referring to people, animals, or things usually end in -a:

  una chica *a girl*   **la** paloma *the dove*   **la** silla *the chair*

■ **3.1.3** But many nouns with different endings such as -**e** or with the consonants -**l**, -**r**, -**z**, -**d**, -**n**, -**s** can be either masculine or feminine, and they have to be learned as individual items. The easiest way to remember is to learn each noun with its article:

  un coche *a car*   **un** café *a coffee*
  la ciudad *the town*   **el** tenedor *the fork*

3.2 Natural Gender

■ **3.2.1** Some nouns that refer specifically either to the male or the female gender have completely different forms for the masculine and for the feminine:

  el hombre *the man*   la mujer *the woman*
  el padre *the father*   la madre *the mother*

■ **3.2.2** Other nouns end in **-o** in the masculine form and change the ending into **-a** in the feminine form:

    el niñ**o** *the boy*   la niñ**a** *the girl*

■ **3.2.3** Those that finish in the consonant **d, l, n, r, s, z** add an **-a** at the end of the masculine form to make the feminine:

    el profesor *the teacher* (m)   la profesor**a** *the teacher* (f)

■ **3.2.4** Some nouns have the same form for masculine and feminine. In this case we can only recognize which gender they belong to from the other words that accompany them, such as the article or adjectives or pronouns, as these will have either a masculine or a feminine form. These are:

a Nouns ending in **-a** and **-sta**
    el atlet**a** *the athlete* (m)   la atlet**a** *the athlete* (f)
    el art**ista** *the artist* (m)   la art**ista** *the artist* (f)

b Nouns ending in **-nte**:
    el estudia**nte**   *the student* (m)
    la estudia**nte**   *the student* (f)

    But some nouns ending in **-nte** change to **-nta** (change the **-e** into **-a**) in the feminine:
    el dependie**nte**   *the store clerk* (m)
    la dependie**nta**   *the store clerk* (f)

c Nouns ending in **-e**, apart from those mentioned above, are either invariable: **el/la intérprete** (*the interpreter*), or variable: **el jefe/la jefa** (*the boss*).

d Many nouns that refer to professions tend to keep the masculine form when they refer to the feminine, and only the article or adjectives and pronouns accompanying the noun change:
    el médico *the doctor* (m)   **la** médico *the doctor* (f)

However, as more women take on jobs traditionally held by men, feminine forms are evolving:

el arquitect**o**	*the architect* (m)
la arquitect**a**	*the architect* (f)

■ **3.2.5** A few nouns have special endings for the feminine.

a Nouns that end in **-or (-tor, -dor)** adopt the ending **-triz** for the feminine form:

el ac**tor** *the actor* la ac**triz** *the actress*

b A few others, less common, add **-esa** or **-isa**:

el príncipe *the prince* la princ**esa** *the princess*

■ **3.2.6** Some nouns that have either feminine or masculine gender can be applied to either males or females:

el bebé (*the baby*), **la persona** (*the person*), **el personaje** (*the character*), **un genio** (*a genius*), **una estrella** (*a star*).

■ **3.2.7** Summary—Natural Gender

o	~	a	niño	~	niña
Consonant +		a	profesor	~	profesora
Different word			**padre**	~	**madre**
Same word			estudiante	~	estudiante
			periodista	~	periodista

3.3 Grammatical Gender

Nouns that refer to objects are always the same gender. They are either feminine or masculine.

■ **3.3.1** Summary—Grammatical Gender

ending	gender	example
-o	= masculine	**el** libro (*the book*)
-a	= feminine	**la** mesa (*the table*)
-e	= arbitrary	**el** café (*the coffee*)
		la leche (*the milk*)
-consonant: arbitrary (the majority are masculine)		**el** autobús (*the bus*)
But many ending in **-d, -z,** and **-l** are feminine		**la** sal (*the salt*)

■ **3.3.2** Irregular Nouns

a A few nouns ending in **-o** are feminine:
   la mano *the hand*   **la** radio *the radio*

b Some words ending in **-ma** are masculine:
   el problema *the problem* **el** clima *the climate*

3.4 Number: Singular and Plural

In Spanish nouns can be singular and plural. The plural is formed by adding **-s** or **-es** to the singular.

■ **3.4.1** An **-s** is added to nouns ending in a vowel:
   el apartamento   **los** apartamentos
   the apartment   *the apartments*

■ **3.4.2** An **-es** is added to nouns ending in a consonant:
   el tren *the train*   **los** trenes *the trains*

3.5 Singular and Plural—Special Cases

■ **3.5.1** Nouns ending in **-í** or **-ú** add **-es** to the plural:
   el paquistaní *Pakistani*   **los** paquistaníes *Pakistanis*

■ **3.5.2** Nouns ending in -s preceded by a nonstressed vowel do not change for the plural:

el lunes *on Monday*   **los** lunes *on Mondays*

But this is not the case if the -s is preceded by a stressed vowel:

el autobús *the bus*   los autobus**es** *the buses*

■ **3.5.3** Mixed gender groups—two or more masculine and feminine nouns occurring in a mixed group always adopt the masculine plural form:

los padres   *the parents*
los niños   *children (boys and girls)*

4 Word Formation

4.1 Suffixes

Suffixes are endings that can be added to the end of a word to modify its meaning. Not all words take suffixes.

■ **4.1.1** Some suffixes add a special meaning to the word. They often refer to size, but they can also reflect emotions, affection, and intensity. They are:

Augmentative *big, great big* *very, extremely*	**-ón** **-ote** **-ísimo**	cabez**ón**, *stubborn* grand**ote**, *very big* car**ísimo**, *extremely* *expensive*
Diminutive *small, little*	**-ito/a, -illo/a,** **-ico/a**	mes**ita**, *little table* niñ**ito**, *little child*
Pejorative *horrible/bad*	**-ucha**	cas**ucha**, *horrible* *house*

See 8.3 for **-ísimo** (superlatives).

■ **4.1.2** Suffixes indicate profession or occupation or places of work:

| panad**ero** | *baker* |
| zapat**ería** | *shoestore* |

4.2 Prefixes

Prefixes go before the word and also give extra meaning to it. They can be added to verbs, nouns, and adjectives:

superdotado	*brainy*
antibelicista	*conscientious objector*
exmarido	*ex-husband*

5 The Definite Article

Articles are words that accompany nouns and go before them. They give a more concrete meaning to a noun. In English the definite article is *the*. In Spanish, articles show whether nouns are feminine or masculine and singular or plural. This is very useful when the endings of the nouns are not obvious.

5.1 Form and Meaning

■ **5.1.1** In Spanish there are four different words for *the*. There is also a neuter article **lo** (for uses of **lo** see 5.4).

	Definite Article (*the*)		
	Masculine	Feminine	Neuter
singular	**el**	**la**	**lo**
plural	**los**	**las**	

El restaurante está cerrado.   *The restaurant is closed.*
La estación está a la derecha.   *The station is on the right.*
Los chicos están en la calle.   *The boys are in the street.*
Las bebidas están servidas.   *The drinks are served.*

■ **5.1.2** **El** can be used with feminine nouns instead of **la** when these start with the stressed vowel **a** or **ha** (note the **h** is silent):

El agua está fría.   *The water is cold.*
El hambre es una lacra   *Hunger is a disease of our*
de nuestra sociedad.   *society.*

This does not happen in the plural when **las** is used:

Las aguas de este río   *The water in this river is*
están contaminadas.   *polluted.*

5.2 Prepositions + the Definite Article

When the article **el** is preceded by the preposition **a** the result is the contracted form **al**. If it is preceded by **de** the form is **del**. These are the only two cases of word contraction in Spanish:

Fui **al** cine ayer.   *I went **to the** movies yesterday.*
Juan salió **del** banco.   *Juan left **the** bank.*

5.3 Uses and Omissions

■ **5.3.1** The definite article is used before the noun. It helps determine the noun, especially with regard to gender and number in the many cases where it is not clear from the noun itself:

El chico llegó a **la** ciudad   *The boy arrived in town*
ayer.   *yesterday.*

■ **5.3.2** It must be used with abstract and generic nouns: **la naturaleza** (*nature*), **el amor** (*love*), **la sociedad** (*society*), **la educación** (*education*):

La educación de adultos   *Adult education is very*
es muy importante.   *important.*

■ **5.3.3** It must also be used with general nouns that indicate belonging to a certain group or category. These can be in the singular—**la mujer** (*women*), **la gente** (*people*), **el vino** (*wine*):

El vino chileno es bueno.   *Chilean **wine** is good.*
La gente de aquí es muy   ***People** here are very nice.*
simpática.

and in the plural—**los mexicanos** (*Mexicans*), **los niños** (*children*):

Hoy en día **los niños** no   *Nowadays **children** don't do*
hacen mucho ejercicio.   *much exercise.*

■ **5.3.4** It is used before titles—**señor** (*Mr.*), **señora**

(*Mrs./Ms.*), **doctor** (*doctor*):

El señor Pérez y **la** señora Martínez están en una reunión.

Mr. Pérez and Ms. Martínez are in a meeting.

But the article is not used when addressing the person directly:

Señor Ramos, ¿puede venir a mi oficina?

Mr. Ramos, can you come to my office?

■ **5.3.5** The article is also used before names of family— **abuelo** (*grandfather*), **tía** (*aunt*):

Llama a **la** abuela. *Call grandmother.*

But it is not used with **papá** (*dad*) or **mamá** (*mom*):

Dile a mamá que ha llamado papá.

Tell Mom that Dad has phoned.

■ **5.3.6** It is used with names of sports teams:

El Barcelona ganó la copa. *Barcelona won the cup.*

■ **5.3.7** It is generally used before names of languages:

Me gusta **el** español. *I like Spanish.*

The article is not used before the name of a language:

a after **hablar** (*to speak*), **saber** (*to know*), and **aprender** (*to learn*):

No **hablo** inglés. *I don't speak English.*

b after the preposition **en**:

Está hablando **en** catalán. *He is speaking in Catalan.*

■ **5.3.8** The article is used with days of the week:

La clase empieza **el** lunes. *The class will start on Monday.*

But it is not used with days in dates:

| Hoy es miércoles, | *Today is Wednesday,* |
| 8 de mayo. | *May 8th.* |

■ **5.3.9** It is used with time expressions and before numerals:

| Es **la** una. | *It's one o'clock.* |
| Vivo en **el** número 18. | *I live at number 18.* |

But the article is not used in Spanish with ordinal numbers in titles for kings, popes, etc.:

| Juan Carlos primero | *Juan Carlos **the** First* |

■ **5.3.10** It is used when expressing measurement and weight:

| Cuesta 10 pesos **el** | *It costs 10 pesos a/per* |
| kilo/**el** litro/**el** metro. | *kilo/liter/meter.* |

■ **5.3.11** With parts of the body and clothes the definite article is used instead of the possessive adjective:

| Lávate **las** manos. | *Wash your hands.* |
| Ponte **los** guantes. | *Put your gloves on.* |

■ **5.3.12** With names of some countries the general tendency is to omit the article: en **Estados Unidos** (*in the United States*), en **Alemania** (*in Germany*).
But there are exceptions where you will see the article used:

El Salvador	*El Salvador*
El Reino Unido	*UK*
La India	*India*

and when the noun is qualified with extra information:

| **La** España de hoy | *present-day Spain* |

■ **5.3.13** Some common phrases that express place need an article in Spanish—**a la escuela** (*to school*), **en la escuela** (*in school*), **en el trabajo** (*at work*), **en la iglesia** (*in church*), **en la cárcel** (*in prison*), **en la televisión** (*on television*), **en el mar** (*at sea*):

Voy a **la** escuela.	*I'm going to school.*
Está en **el** trabajo.	*He is at work.*
Veo **la** televisión.	*I watch television.*

■ **5.3.14** The word **casa** in Spanish has two meanings: *house*, *home*. The article is used when **casa** means *house*:

Entró en **la** casa sin llamar.	*She went into **the** house without calling.*

But the article is not used when **casa** means *home*:

Voy a casa.	*I'm going home.*

5.4 The Neuter Article *Lo*

The neuter article **lo** accompanies adjectives and is used in whole sentences. It does not accompany nouns.

An adjective preceded by **lo** becomes an abstract noun. In English it is often translated by *things*:

Lo peor de este sitio es el clima.	*The worst thing about this place is the climate.*
Lo nuevo no siempre es bueno.	*New things are not always good.*
Lo que me contaste ayer no es verdad.	*What you told me yesterday is not true.*

6   The Indefinite Article

6.1 Form and Meaning

■ **6.1.1** In Spanish there are four different words for *a* and *an*.

| | Indefinite Article (*a, an*) | |
	Masculine	Feminine
singular	**un**	**una**
plural	**unos**	**unas**

¿Hay **un** restaurante por aquí?	*Is there **a** restaurant around here?*
Luis trabaja en **una** tienda.	*Luis works in **a** shop.*
¿Quieres **unas** tapas?	*Would you like **some** snacks?*
¿Tienes **unos** minutos?	*Have you got a **few** minutes?*

■ **6.1.2** As with the definite article, the indefinite article **un** is used with feminine nouns instead of **una** when these have a stressed vowel **a** or **ha** at the beginning of the word (note the **h** is silent in **ha**):

Un agua mineral, por favor.	**A** *mineral water, please.*
Ésta es **un** área turística.	*This is **a** tourist area.*

■ **6.1.3** Meanings of **unos, unas**

- *approximately*:

Ganó **unos** dos millones en la lotería.	*She won **approximately** two million in the lottery.*

- *some* or *a few*:

¿Quieres **unos** caramelos?	*Would you like **some** candy?*
Leí **unos** libros.	*I read **a few** books.*

- *a pair of* (with objects such as **pantalones** [*pants*], **gafas** [*glasses*], etc.):

He comprado **unos**   *I've bought **a pair of** pants*
pantalones y **unas** gafas. *and **a pair of** glasses.*

6.2 Uses and Omissions

■ 6.2.1 The indefinite article is used to accompany nouns that are unknown to the speaker or when it is unimportant whether or not they are known to the speaker:

Una chica ha venido a verte. *A girl has come to see you.*
¿Tienes **un** bolígrafo?   *Have you got **a** pen?*

■ 6.2.2 It helps to distinguish nouns from adjectives:

Es extranjero.   *It is foreign.*
Es **un** extranjero.   *He is **a** foreigner.*

■ 6.2.3 It is needed to add emphasis:

¡Es **un** tonto!   *He is stupid!*

■ 6.2.4 It is used before nouns indicating profession and social status that are followed by an adjective or a qualifying phrase:

Es **un** profesor excelente. *He's **an** excellent teacher.*

Remember, however, that in Spanish the indefinite article is not used before nouns indicating professions except in the cases mentioned above:

Soy profesor.   *I'm **a** teacher.*

■ 6.2.5 The indefinite article is not used:

a in exclamations after words like ¡**qué** . . . !
(*what a . . . !*) and **tal** (*such*); and with **medio** (*half*),
cierto (*certain*), and **otro** (*another*):

¡**Qué** casa tan bonita!   *What **a** beautiful house!*
Quiero **medio** kilo de   *I would like half **a** kilo (about 2*
queso.   *½ pounds) of cheese.*

b in exclamatory expressions such as:

¡Es mentira!   *It's **a** lie!*

c with the numbers **cien** (*a hundred*), **mil** (*a thousand*), and other numerical expressions such as **media docena** (*half a dozen*):

Esto cuesta **mil** pesos.   *This costs **a** thousand pesos.*

d after the verbs **llevar** (*to wear*), **usar** (*to use*), **buscar** (*to look for*), and **comprar** (*to buy*):

Luis **lleva** sombrero.   *Luis wears **a** hat.*

Ana está **buscando** piso.   *Ana is looking for **an** apartment.*

But it is used if the noun in the sentence is followed by an adjective:

Ana está buscando **un** piso **grande**.   *Ana is looking for **a** big apartment.*

e after expressions with **como** (*as*), **sin** (*without*):

Andrés trabaja **como** ingeniero.   *Andrés works as **an** engineer.*

No salgas **sin** abrigo.   *Don't go out without **a** coat.*

f before singular nouns, when expressing possession:

Tiene coche.   *She has **a** car.*

g with the language of publicity:

Se vende piso.   *Condominium for sale.*

7 Adjectives

Adjectives explain, describe, or say something about a noun. There are various kinds of adjectives that modify nouns in different ways. This section covers the qualifying adjectives, which add a quality to the noun. They are words such as **grande** (*big*), **pequeño** (*small*), **norteamericano** (*American*), **mexicano** (*Mexican*), etc. Most adjectives occur immediately after the noun:

televisión mexicana	*Mexican television*
vino blanco	*white wine*

7.1 Position Changing Form and Meaning

■ **7.1.1** The following adjectives can occur before the noun. Then their masculine form is shortened as follows:

bueno	> **buen**	*good*
grande	> **gran**	*big/great*
malo	> **mal**	*bad*
santo	> **san**	*saint*
primero	> **primer**	*first*
tercero	> **tercer**	*third*

un chico **bueno**	*a good boy (well-behaved)*
un **buen** chico	*a good boy*
una casa **grande**	*a big house*
una **gran** casa	*a great house*

■ **7.1.2** The feminine form does not change in **buena**, **mala**, **santa**, **primera**, and **tercera** (but it does in **gran**):

una chica **buena** = una **buena** chica

■ **7.1.3** There are other adjectives that, depending on whether they are placed before or after the noun, change their meaning:

antiguo:	mi **antiguo** piso	*my former apartment*
	un piso **antiguo**	*an old apartment*
pobre:	¡**pobre** hombre!	*poor man!*
	Es un hombre **pobre**.	*He's a poor man.*

7.2 Agreement of Adjectives in Number

Adjectives agree in number with the noun. If the noun is plural the adjective must also have a plural form. The rule is the same as for nouns.

| after a vowel | after a consonant (**l, d, n, r**) |
| add **-s** | add **-es** |

el apartamento moderno	*the modern apartment*
los apartamentos modernos	*the modern apartments*
el vestido azul	*the blue dress*
los vestidos azules	*the blue dresses*

But note the few exceptions. Adjectives ending in **-í, -ú** add **-es**. There are very few:

| Israelíes | *Israeli* |
| Hindúes | *Hindu* |

7.3 Agreement of Adjectives in Gender

Adjectives agree in gender with the noun. The masculine ending is **-o** and the feminine is **-a**:

| un vino **bueno** | *a good wine* |
| una comida **buena** | *a good meal* |

■ **7.3.1** Adjectives ending in **-e** or in a consonant (**-l, -r, -n, -z**) do not change, e.g., **feliz** (*happy*), **marrón** (*brown*):

| el pollo **caliente** | *hot chicken* |
| la sopa **caliente** | *hot soup* |

| el abrigo **azul** | *the blue coat* |
| la falda **azul** | *the blue skirt* |

■ **7.3.2** You might find a few adjectives that end in -**a**. They do not change either and can be both masculine and feminine: **hipócrita** (*hypocritical*), **optimista** (*optimist*).

Note also colors that are originally nouns come into this category: **rosa** (*pink*), **naranja** (*orange*), **violeta** (*violet*).

■ **7.3.3** If we want to describe two nouns with the same adjective and one of the nouns is masculine and the other feminine the adjective always adopts the masculine form:

Los chic**os** y chic**as** american**os**.   *American boys and girls.*

7.4 Exceptions in Gender Changes

Some adjectives ending in a consonant, which can also act as nouns, change and follow the rules for nouns. For example, nationalities:

| un chico **inglés** | *an English boy* |
| una chica **inglesa** | *an English girl* |

8 Comparatives and Superlatives

Comparatives and superlatives are used to express different degrees of intensity, quantity, or quality through expressions such as **más/menos** . . . **que** (*more/less . . . than*), **tan/tanto** . . . **como** (*as . . . as*).
There are comparatives and superlatives of adjectives, nouns, adverbs, and verbs.

8.1 Comparatives of Adjectives

Adjectives of quality can express different grades of comparison. The comparative is formed by adding **más** (*more*), **menos** (*less*), or **tan** (*as*) before the adjective. This is followed by **que** (*than*) or **como** (*as*).

■ **8.1.1** Forms of the comparatives:

más . . . que	menos . . . que	tan . . . como

Juan es **más** alto **que** Pedro. *Juan is taller than Pedro.*
Este hotel es **menos** lujoso **que** aquél. *This hotel is less luxurious than that one.*
El camping es **tan** cómodo **como** el hotel. *The campsite is as comfortable as the hotel.*

■ **8.1.2** In comparisons with two or more adjectives, **más**, **menos**, and **tan** are not repeated before each adjective:
Tú casa es **más** grande y bonita **que** la mía. *Your house is bigger and prettier than mine.*

■ **8.1.3** In sentences with the verb **ser** (*to be*), it is common not to repeat **ser** in the second part of the comparison:
La película es **tan** interesante **como** divertida. *The film is as interesting as it is amusing.*

8.2 Irregular Comparative Forms

Some adjectives have irregular comparative forms:

bueno	*good*	**mejor**	*better*
malo	*bad*	**peor**	*worse*
grande	*big*	**mayor**	*bigger*
pequeño	*small*	**menor**	*smaller*

They are followed by **que** in the comparative:

Este vino es **mejor que** el que tomamos ayer. — *This wine is **better than** the one we drank yesterday.*

Luis tiene quince años; es **mayor que** Juan. — *Luis is fifteen; he's **older than** Juan.*

■ **8.2.1** These irregular comparatives are often substituted by their equivalent regular comparatives, especially in the case of **grande** (*big*) and **pequeño** (*small*) referring to size:

Tu coche es **más grande que** el mío. — *Your car is **bigger than** mine.*

■ **8.2.2** **Mayor** and **menor** are used more when expressing age (*older, younger*):

Tengo un hermano **mayor que** yo y una hermana **menor**. — *I have a brother **older than** I and a **younger** sister.*

■ **8.2.3** **Mejor** (*better*) and **peor** (*worse*) can also be used as adverbs; they act as comparatives of **bien** (*well*) and **mal** (*badly*).

Canta **mejor que** antes. — *He sings **better than** before.*

Juan está **peor que** ayer. Tiene fiebre. — *Juan is **worse than** yesterday. He has a temperature.*

■ **8.2.4** The expression **igual que** (*the same as*) is also used as a comparative. It can also have a plural form—**iguales que**.

Esta camisa es **igual que** la tuya. — *This shirt is **the same as** yours.*

8.3 Superlatives of Adjectives

■ **8.3.1** The superlative form of the adjective is formed with **más** or **menos** preceded by the definite article **el/la/los/las** (*the*):

el/la . . . más . . . de
el/la . . . menos . . . de

Este abrigo es **el más** caro **de** todos.	*This overcoat is **the most** expensive **of** all.*
Esta ciudad es **la menos** interesante **del** viaje.	*This city is **the least** interesting **of** the trip.*

■ **8.3.2** The superlative can be formed by adding the suffix **-ísimo, -ísima** and the plural **-ísimos, -ísimas**:

Este libro es **interesantísimo.**	*This book is **very interesting**.*

■ **8.3.3** There are some special superlative forms:

el más grande	=	**máximo**	*the biggest*
el más pequeño	=	**mínimo**	*the smallest*
el mejor	=	**óptimo**	*the best*
el peor	=	**pésimo**	*the worst*

El precio **mínimo** de la entrada es de mil pesos.	*The **lowest** price of a ticket is a thousand pesos.*

8.4 Comparatives of Numerals or Quantities

Note the difference between **más de** and **más que** in a negative sentence. If **más de** is used, we want to express the maximum number. If **más que** is used, we mean that we expected more:

No hay **más de** veinte estudiantes en la clase.	*There aren't more than twenty students in the class.*

No hay **más que** veinte
estudiantes en la clase.

*There are only twenty students
in the class.*

8.5 Special Constructions

más/menos . . . + que + el (la/los/las) que:

Este coche es **más** grande
que el que vimos ayer.

*This car is smaller than the one
we saw yesterday.*

más/menos . . . + de + el (la/los/las) que:

Tiene **menos** años **de los
que** aparenta.

He's younger than he looks.

más/menos + de lo que:

Cuesta **menos de lo que** crees. *It costs less than you think.*

See section 13 on relative pronouns for a study of **el que/la
que/lo que**.

8.6 Comparatives of Nouns

These are formed in the same way as the comparatives of
adjectives, except for **tan**, which becomes **tanto** before a
noun. **Tanto** changes in gender and number and is translated
as *as much, as many, so much,* or *so many,* depending on the
context:

Tiene **más** dinero **que** yo.

*He has **more** money **than** I have.*

No tengo **tanta** suerte
como tú.

*I don't have **as much** luck
as you.*

8.7 Comparatives of Verbs

The comparatives of verbs are formed in the same way as
those of nouns. **Tanto** used with verbs can be translated as
as much as, as little as:

Juan estudia **más que**
(estudiaba) el año pasado.

*Juan studies **more than** last
year.*

See 17.10 for comparison of adverbs.

9 Personal Pronouns

Personal pronouns are used to substitute the names of people or objects in the sentence and they vary in form according to gender and number.

There are two kinds of personal pronouns: subject pronouns and object pronouns. Subject pronouns are words like *I, you, he, she, it, we,* or *they.* Object pronouns are words like *me, him, her, us,* or *them.*

9.1 Forms of Subject Pronouns

In Spanish all subject pronouns vary according to number. They also change gender except in the first and second person singular:

	singular		plural	
person	masculine	feminine	masculine	feminine
1st *I, we*	yo		nosotros	nosotras
2nd (familiar) *you*	tú*		vosotros*	vosotras*
2nd (formal) *you*	usted (Ud./Vd.)		ustedes (Uds./Vds.)	
3rd *he, she, they*	él	ella	ellos	ellas

*See 9.4.5 for regional usage.

There is a neuter form in the third person singular: **ello** (*it*). The written forms of **usted** and **ustedes** are usually abbreviated: **usted** = Ud./Vd., **ustedes** = Uds./Vds.

When there are two speakers, one male and one female, the personal pronoun in the masculine plural form is used:

Ellos (María y Juan) tienen un apartamento precioso.   *They (María and Juan) have a beautiful apartment.*

9.2 Position of Subject Pronouns

In general subject pronouns do not follow a fixed order in sentences. They usually go before the verb and at the beginning of the sentence.

■ **9.2.1** In questions, they are usually placed after the verb:

¿Vas **tú** o voy **yo**?	*Are **you** going or am **I** going?*

The same occurs with reported speech:

–¡Trabaja más!– gritó **ella** enfadada.	*"Work harder!" **she** shouted angrily.*

And with the imperative:

¡Dúchate **tú** primero!	***You** take a shower first!*

■ **9.2.2** Subject pronouns can be combined with **mismo/a, propio/a, solo/a**:

a for emphasis:

Viajo **yo sola**.	*I am traveling **on my own**.*

b to indicate the gender:

¡Hazlo **tú mismo**!	*Do it **yourself**!*

■ **9.2.3** They can be combined with numerals:

Este chalet es para **nosotros cuatro**.	*This chalet is for **us four**.*

and other pronouns of an indefinite nature:

Presentamos el programa para **todos ustedes**.	*We present this program for **you all**.*

9.3 Use of Subject Pronouns

■ **9.3.1** Subject pronouns are normally used for emphasis and clarity. In conversation they are usually omitted as the verb endings clearly indicate the person speaking:

Quiero un café, por favor.	*I'd like a coffee, please.*

■ **9.3.2** They are used to avoid confusion between the first and the third person of the verb when these forms coincide:

Todos los días **yo iba** al mercado mientras **él iba** a la playa.

*Every day **I** used to go to the market while **he** went to the beach.*

■ **9.3.3** They are used to emphasize the opposition or contrast between the people who take part in the conversation:

Yo no puedo ir, pero **tú** sí.

*I can't go, but **you** can!*

■ **9.3.4** They are used when the pronoun stands alone, in answer to a question:

¿Quién es? **Yo.**

*Who is it? **Me.** (Literally: I)*

¿Quién ha hecho esto? **Ella.**

*Who's done this? **She** has.*

■ **9.3.5** The neuter form **ello** (*it, that*) is hardly used in speech. Although it might be encountered in written texts of a more formal kind, the tendency is to substitute it with the demonstrative pronoun **eso**.

Ello always refers to an idea, and not to a concrete noun.

No tiene dinero, pero **ello** no le impide divertirse.

*She has no money, but **that** does not stop her from enjoying herself.*

9.4 Use of *Tú* and *Usted*

■ **9.4.1** The form **usted** is used in formal situations or when addressing someone you do not know unless he or she is a very young person or a child.

■ **9.4.2** **Tú** is used with children, family, or someone you know well and when you are invited to do so by the person you are addressing.

In Spain there is a notable tendency now to use **tú** from the first meeting. It is particularly noticeable among young people.

■ **9.4.3** **Usted** and **ustedes** are often used to stress the polite tone or to avoid confusion with the third person when it is not clear from the context who is being referred to.

¿Es **usted** vegetariano?　　*Are you a vegetarian?*

■ **9.4.4** It is important to remember that the formal use of the second person is formed with the third person endings, singular or plural, of the verbs concerned: **usted puede** (*you can*), **ustedes pueden** (*you can*).

Señor González, **usted**　　*You can sleep in this room,*
puede dormir en esta　　*Mr. González.*
habitación.

■ **9.4.5** The more informal forms of **tú** and **vosotros** (*you*, singular and plural) are often replaced by **usted** and **ustedes** in Latin America even in informal situations among family and friends. This is also the case in parts of southern Spain and in the Canaries. In Argentina, Uruguay, and Paraguay **vos** is used instead of **tú** and **ti**:

Están hablando de **vos**.　　*They are talking about you.*

9.5 Personal Pronouns with Prepositions

■ **9.5.1** The personal pronouns studied above can all be accompanied by prepositions, mostly without changing their form:

El vino es **para él**.　　*The wine is **for him**.*
¿Vienes **con nosotros**?　　*Are you coming **with us**?*

But **yo** and **tú** adopt different forms after a preposition— **yo** becomes **mí** and **tú** becomes **ti**:

La paella es **para mí/para ti**.　　*The paella is **for me/for you**.*

■ **9.5.2** However, there are two prepositions with which
yo and **tú** stay the same: **entre** (*between*) and **según**
(*according to*):

Podemos limpiar la casa **entre tú** y **yo**.	*We can clean the house, **you** *and **I**.
Según tú, no hay problemas.	***According to you**, there are no problems.*

■ **9.5.3** If **yo** and **tú** are accompanied by the preposition
con (*with*), they become special forms—**con** + **yo** =
conmigo (*with me*) and **con** + **tú** = **contigo** (*with you*):

¿Quieres ir al cine **conmigo**?	*Do you want to go to the movies **with me**?*
No puedo salir **contigo** hoy.	*I cannot go out **with you** today.*

■ **9.5.4** The prepositions **a** or **de** plus **él** (*he*) do not contract
as **él** is a stressed form: **a él**, **de él**. Do not confuse **él** with
the article **el** (*the*):

No he visto a Juan últimamente. No sé nada **de él**.	*I haven't seen Juan recently. I have no news **of him**.*

■ **9.5.5** The Forms **sí** and **consigo**

a In the third person when we want to refer to *him* or *her*
as *himself* or *herself* preceded by a preposition, the form
to use is **sí** often accompanied by **mismo/misma**. It has
a reflexive character:

Habla **para sí (mismo)**.	*He talks **to himself**.*
Ana está satisfecha **de sí misma**.	*Ana is pleased **with herself**.*

b If **sí** is preceded by the preposition **con** (*with*), then
con + **sí** becomes **consigo** (*with him/herself*):

Juan está contento **consigo mismo**.	*Juan is pleased with himself.*

c These forms do not always have a reflexive meaning.
The meaning is different if the preposition **entre**
(*between/among*) is added. **Entre sí** can mean *among*
themselves in sentences such as:

Las niñas hablan español **entre sí.**	*The girls speak Spanish* ***among themselves.***

d The form **sí** is often substituted by **él/ellos** or **ella/ellas**:

El cree que el dinero es **para él (mismo)/para sí.**	*He thinks the money is* ***for*** *himself.*
Las niñas hablan español **entre ellas.**	*The girls speak Spanish* ***among*** *themselves.*

9.6 Object Pronouns

These are divided into direct and indirect object pronouns.
They are words like *me, you, him, her, us, them.*

■ **9.6.1** The first and second persons are the same for
direct and indirect object pronouns: **me** (*me*), **te** (*you*—
informal), and plural **nos** (*us*) and **os** (*you*—informal).

Te veré en la fiesta. (direct object)	*I'll see* ***you*** *at the party.*
Nos dio un libro. (indirect object)	*He gave* ***us*** *a book.*

■ **9.6.2** Third Person Object Pronouns

a The third person has different forms for the direct and
indirect object pronouns:

¿Llamaste a Juan? Sí, **lo** llamé ayer.	*Did you call Juan? Yes, I called* ***him*** *yesterday.*
¿Escribiste una carta a Juan? Sí, **le** escribí una carta.	*Did you write a letter to Juan? Yes, I wrote* ***him*** *a letter.*

b The direct object pronouns have different forms for
feminine and masculine: **lo** (*him, it, you*—formal) for the

masculine singular and **la** (*her, it, you*—formal) for the feminine singular, with **los** (*them, you*—formal) and **las** (*them, you*—formal) for the plurals:

¿Viste a mi madre?	*Did you see my mother?*
Sí, **la** vi.	*Yes, I saw **her**.*
¿Viste a mis padres?	*Did you see my parents?*
Sí, **los** vi.	*Yes, I saw **them**.*

There is a neuter **lo** (*it*), which is studied in 9.6.3.

c The indirect object pronouns in the third person are the same for feminine and masculine: **le** (*him, her*) for the singular and **les** (*them*) for the plural.

■ 9.6.3 Direct Object Pronouns

	singular			plural	
person	masculine	feminine	neuter	masculine	feminine
1st	**me** (*me*)			**nos** (*us*)	
2nd	**te** (*you*)			**os** (*you*)	
3rd	**lo** (*him*)	**la** (*her*)	**lo** (*it*)	**los** (*them*)	**las** (*them*)

Me saluda todos los días.	*He greets **me** every day.*
Te quiero.	*I love **you**.*
Juan **nos** llamó ayer.	*Juan called **us** yesterday.*
¿**Lo** quiere?	*Do you want **it**?*
Señor Pérez, **lo** llaman.	*Mr. Pérez, they are calling **you**.*

■ 9.6.4 Indirect Object Pronouns

	singular	plural
person	masculine feminine	masculine feminine
1st	me (me)	nos (us)
2nd	te (you)	os (you)
3rd	le/se (him/her/you)	les/se (them)

¿**Te** mandó una postal?	*Did she send **you** a card?*
Le compraré un regalo.	*I will buy **him/her** a present.*
Señora García, **le** traen un paquete.	*Mrs. García, they are bringing a package for **you**.*

9.7 Position of Object Pronouns

■ **9.7.1** Object pronouns go before the verb:

Juan **me** invitó a pasar unos días con él.
*Juan invited **me** to spend a few days with him.*

■ **9.7.2** They follow the verb when it is in the infinitive, imperative, or gerund (-*ing*) form. In these cases they are attached to the verb:

Quiero comprar**lo**.	*I want to buy **it**.*
¡Cóme**lo**!	*Eat **it**!*
La ducha está rota. Están reparándo**la**.	*The shower is broken. They are repairing **it**.*

■ **9.7.3** When the pronoun is attached to the verb the stress of the word changes place and often needs an accent:

Toma la medicina.	*Take the medicine.*
Tóma**la**.	*Take **it**.*

■ **9.7.4** If the infinitive or the gerund depend on another verb it is possible to put the pronoun before the main verb:

Lo quiero comprar.   *I want to buy **it**.*
¿**Nos** puedes decir la hora? *Can you tell **us** the time?*
Nos están llamando.   *They are calling **us**.*

■ **9.7.5** When a direct object pronoun is used in combination with a subject personal pronoun the subject pronoun precedes the object pronoun:

Yo lo tomo sin azúcar.   *I take **it** without sugar.*
Nosotros os llevaremos.   ***We** will take **you**.*

■ **9.7.6** If **le** or **les** is used together with **lo** or **la**, **le** and **les** become **se**, which is placed before **lo** or **la**:

Doy el libro a Juan.   *I give the book to Juan.*
Se lo doy.   *I give **it** to **him**.*
Compré un regalo para   *I bought a present for the*
los niños. **Se lo** compré. *children. I bought **it** for **them**.*

■ **9.7.7** If two object pronouns appear together the indirect pronoun **me**, **te**, **nos**, **os**, **se** always comes first:

Te mandé una postal.   *I sent you a postcard.*
Te la mandé.   *I sent **it** to **you**.*

■ **9.7.8** **Me** (indirect object) always follows **te** and **se** (direct object) when they appear together:

Se me escapó el tren.   *The train left without me.*
Espera, no **te me** vayas.   *Wait, don't walk out on me.*

■ **9.7.9** Summary—Personal Pronoun Word Order

Subject + indirect object + direct object + verb			
yo	**te**	**lo**	**compro**
I	*for you*	*it*	*buy*

9.8 Uses of *Lo, Le, La,* and Their Plural Forms

■ **9.8.1** Lo, los are always used as direct object pronouns for objects that are masculine:

¿Comprarás el periódico?	*Will you buy the paper?*
Sí, **lo** compraré.	*Yes, I will buy it.*
¿Comprarás los sellos?	*Will you buy the stamps?*
Sí, **los** compraré.	*Yes, I will buy them.*

and also for males:

Lo vi ayer (a Juan).	*I saw him (Juan) yesterday.*
Los vi ayer (a Juan y a Luis).	*I saw them (Juan and Luis) yesterday.*

■ **9.8.2** Lo, los are often substituted by le, les in the case of male persons (this is called **Leísmo**):

Le vi ayer.	*I saw him yesterday.*

Both **lo, los** and **le, les** are now accepted as correct and they are often mixed up in conversation by the same person:

Lo llamé y **le** invité a cenar.	*I called him and invited him to dinner.*

■ **9.8.3** La, las are always used as the direct object pronoun for an object that is feminine:

¿Comprarás la casa?	*Will you buy the house?*
Sí, **la** compraré.	*Yes, I will buy it.*
¿Comprarás las botas?	*Will you buy the boots?*
Sí, **las** compraré.	*Yes, I will buy them.*

and also for females:

La vi ayer (a María).	*I saw her (María) yesterday.*
Las vi ayer (a María y a Ana).	*I saw them (María and Ana) yesterday.*

■ **9.8.4** The indirect object pronouns **le, les** are not used for objects but they are used both for males and females:

Le escribiré una carta (a Juan). *I will write **him** a letter (to Juan).*

Le mandaré una postal (a María). *I will send **her** a postcard (to María).*

Sometimes **la, las** are used instead of **le, les** for females (this is called **Laísmo**); this is not grammatically correct although it is widely used in certain areas of Spain and Latin America.

La escribiré una carta (a María). *I will write a letter to **her** (to María).*

■ **9.8.5** **Le, les** become **se** when they are followed by another personal pronoun:

Se lo regalo. *I give **it to him**.*

The form **se** is ambiguous as it can refer to *him, her, them,* or *you.* It is often reinforced by the special prepositional form **a** plus the personal pronoun or noun to which **se** refers:

Se lo doy a Ana. *I give it to Ana.*
Se lo doy **a ella**. *I give it to **her**.*

There is often an overuse of the personal pronouns in Spanish:

Los zapatos **se los** compré a Juan en esta tienda. *I bought Juan his shoes in this shop.*

9.9 The Neuter *Lo*

The neuter **lo** is used as a direct object when it refers to part of a sentence or to a concept:

¿Dónde está Juan? *Where is Juan?*
No **lo** sé. *I don't know.*
No **lo** comprendo (el problema). *I don't understand (the problem).*

10 Reflexive Pronouns

Reflexive pronouns accompany reflexive verbs. These are verbs where the subject performs an action on itself:

El no **se ha afeitado** hoy.	*He hasn't shaved today.*
Me levanto siempre a las siete.	*I always get up at seven.*

10.1 Form

The forms of the reflexive pronouns are:

me	*myself*
te	*yourself*
se/sí	*himself/herself/itself/yourself* (**usted**)
consigo	*with/to himself, oneself,* etc.
nos	*ourselves*
os	*yourselves*
se/sí	*themselves/yourselves* (**ustedes**)
consigo	*with/to himself, oneself,* etc.

They coincide with those of the object personal pronouns except in the third person **se/sí/consigo**:

Yo **me** ducho con agua fría.	*I shower in cold water.*
Ella **se** baña.	*She has a bath.*
Habla **consigo mismo**.	*He talks to himself.*

■ **10.1.1** It is important not to confuse the reflexive **se** with the personal pronoun **se** (**le**) or the impersonal or passive **se**.

See section 9 for **le** and section 34 for the passive **se**.

See section 9 for **sí** and **mí**.

See 9.7 for position of object pronouns.

For use of reflexive verbs and other pronominal (e.g., reciprocal) verbs, see section 35.

11 Demonstrative Adjectives and Pronouns

Demonstrative adjectives and pronouns (*this, that, these, those*) determine their accompanying nouns or noun phrases. They tell us whether the noun is near or far from the speaker in time or space.

They are basically the same in form and meaning but the pronouns become adjectives if there is a noun present.

11.1 Form and Meaning of Adjectives

There are three categories that vary in gender and in number:

	masculine	feminine	
singular	**este**	**esta**	*this*
	ese	**esa**	*that (near), past*
	aquel	**aquella**	*that (far), distant past*
plural	**estos**	**estas**	*these*
	esos	**esas**	*those (near), past*
	aquellos	**aquellas**	*those (far), distant past*

11.2 Position of Adjectives

The demonstrative adjective is usually placed before the noun:

Este chico vive en **esa** calle.   *This boy lives in that street (nearby).*

Esas mesas están libres.   *Those tables over there are free.*

But it can be placed after the noun when this is preceded by an article, to express emphasis:

El hombre **aquel** vino a verme.   *That man came to see me.*

11.3 Use of Adjectives

■ **11.3.1** **Este, esta**, and their equivalent plural forms are used when the noun determined is near to the speaker in space or time:

Esta comida es excelente.	*This lunch is excellent.*
Mi cumpleaños es **este** mes.	*My birthday is this month.*

■ **11.3.2** Ese, esa, and their equivalent plural forms are used when the noun determined is far from the speaker but nearer to the listener:

¿Puede darme **ese** abrigo, por favor?	*Can you give me that coat, please?*
Nació en 1936. **Ese** año fue malo.	*He was born in 1936. That was a bad year.*

■ **11.3.3** Aquel, aquella, and their equivalent plural forms are used when the noun determined is far from the speaker and the listener:

Aquel edificio es mi hotel.	*That building (over there) is my hotel.*
¡**Aquellas** vacaciones fueron estupendas!	*Those vacations were great! (a long time ago)*

■ **11.3.4** The difference between ese and aquel (*that*) and their equivalent plural, feminine, and neuter forms is subjective, and it often depends on the perception and intention of the speaker.

a With regard to time, **este** usually indicates the present or a recent time while **ese** and **aquel** indicate the past and the remote past, respectively.

b With regard to space, they indicate the immediate vicinity and the farthest point of distance, respectively:

¿Es **ése** tu coche?	*Is that your car (over there)?*
No, es **aquel** coche que está detrás.	*No, it's that car behind it.*

11.4 Form and Meaning of Pronouns

Demonstrative pronouns have the same form as the adjectives both in masculine and feminine and singular and plural. When they are pronouns the forms have accents, except for those of the neuter form, to distinguish them from the adjectives.

There is also a neuter form, which has no accent because there are no neuter adjectives. Note that there is no neuter plural:

	masculine	feminine	neuter
singular	éste	ésta	esto
	ése	ésa	eso
	aquél	aquélla	aquello
plural	éstos	éstas	
	ésos	ésas	
	aquéllos	aquéllas	

■ **11.4.1** The meaning of the demonstrative pronouns is the same as that of the adjectives for the masculine and feminine forms:

¿Quieres **este** queso?   *Do you want **this** cheese?*
No quiero **éste**, prefiero   *I don't want **this one**, I prefer*
ése.   *that one.*

11.5 Use of Pronouns

■ **11.5.1** If we want to refer to two or more things mentioned in a previous sentence, we use the pronouns **aquél/aquélla** to refer to what is mentioned first and

éste/ésta to that mentioned after:

Tengo dos hermanos, Luis, el mayor y Pedro, el menor; **éste** es profesor, **aquél** es electricista.	*I have two brothers, Luis, the eldest and Pedro, the youngest;* **the latter** *is a teacher,* **the former** *is an electrician.*

■ **11.5.2** Sometimes they are used in a derogatory sense:

Pero, ¡qué dice **éste**!	*But, what on earth is* **he (this man)** *saying!*

■ **11.5.3** They are also used to add emphasis and this use is redundant:

¡**Ésta** es una buena paella!	*This is a good paella!*

11.6 Use of Neuter Forms of Pronouns

The neuter forms refer to inanimate objects and actions in a general way without specifying what they are. They cannot refer to people:

¿Qué es **esto**?	*What's* **this**?
¡No hagas **eso**!	*Don't do* **that**!
¿Puedo ver **aquello**, por favor?	*Can I see* **that**, *please?*

The following are some common expressions in which neuter demonstrative pronouns are used:

¡**Eso** es!	*That's it!*
Por **esto**/Por **eso** . . .	*As a result of* **that** . . .
a **eso** de las ocho	*at* **around** *eight*

12 Possessive Adjectives and Pronouns

Possessive adjectives and pronouns determine the noun indicating possession. They are words like *my*, *mine*, *yours*, *his*, *her*, *ours*, or *theirs*.

As in the case of the demonstratives, possessive pronouns can behave as adjectives if they are accompanying the noun. If not, they behave as pronouns and replace the noun. They have three persons and masculine and feminine forms, except in the short forms, and they can be singular and plural.

12.1 Forms of Adjectives

In Spanish the possessive adjectives have two forms, the full form and the short form.

■ **12.1.1** The full forms are **mío**, **míos** (*my*), **tuyo**, **tuyos** (*your*), **suyo**, **suyos** (*his/her*), and their feminine forms.

■ **12.1.2** The short forms are **mi** (*my*), **tu** (*yours*), and **su** (*his/her*), which do not change form with the gender of the noun. These are short forms of **mío**, **tuyo**, **suyo**, and their feminine forms.

■ **12.1.3** The plural forms, **nuestro**, **nuestros** (*our*), **vuestro**, **vuestros** (*your*), do not have a short form.

■ **12.1.4** Number and gender agreement is determined by the number and gender of the noun possessed:
¿Dónde están **mis** llaves?   *Where are my keys?*
La male**ta suya** es la verde. *His suitcase is the green one.*

■ **12.1.5** The following is a full table of possessive adjectives:

		1st person		2nd person		3rd person	
		before noun	after noun	before noun	after noun	before noun	after noun
possessor one person	m. singular	mi	mío	tu*	tuyo*	su	suyo
	f.		mía		tuya*		suya
	m. plural	mis	míos	tus*	tuyos*	sus	suyos
	f.		mías		tuyas*		suyas
possessor more than one person	m. singular	nuestro		vuestro*		su	suyo
	f.	nuestra		vuestra*			suya
	m. plural	nuestros		vuestros*		sus	suyos
	f.	nuestras		vuestras*			suyas

*See 12.2.5 for regional usage.

12.2 Use and Position of Adjectives

■ **12.2.1** The possessive adjective usually precedes the noun and when this is the case the short forms **mi/tu/su/mis/tus/sus** must be used. These forms cannot be used after the noun:

| **mi** libro | *my book* |
| **tu** casa | *your house* |

■ **12.2.2** The full forms of the adjective **mío/tuyo/suyo** and their feminine and plural forms always appear after the noun:

| No he tenido noticias **suyas**. | *I haven't had **his/her** news.* |
| La blusa **tuya** es más bonita. | ***Your** blouse is nicer.* |

■ **12.2.3** The forms **nuestro/a**, **vuestro/a**, and their plurals can appear before or after the noun. In the latter case the noun might or might not be preceded by an article:

Estos son **nuestros** amigos.	*These are **our** friends.*
Hemos recibido carta **vuestra.**	*We have received **your** letter.*
¿Es éste **el** coche **vuestro**?	*Is this **your** car?*

■ **12.2.4** When the full forms are used the translation in English is *of mine/yours/his/ours/yours/theirs*:

Este hijo **tuyo** es muy travieso.	*This son **of yours** is very naughty.*
Fueron a visitarlos unos amigos **suyos.**	*Some friends **of theirs** went to visit them.*

■ **12.2.5** In Latin American Spanish **tu**, **tuyo/a**, **vuestro/a**, and their plural forms are not used, as the personal pronouns **tú** and **vosotros/as** (singular and plural, informal forms) are not used much. **Su/suyo** and their plural forms are used both in familiar and more formal language.

12.3 Forms of Possessive Pronouns

Possessive pronouns replace the noun and are sometimes preceded by the article. They must agree with the gender and number of the noun replaced.

■ **12.3.1** The following is a table showing the forms of the possessive pronouns:

		1st person	2nd person	3rd person
possessor one person	singular m.	**el mío**	**el tuyo***	**el suyo**
	f.	**la mía**	**la tuya***	**la suya**
	plural m.	**los míos**	**los tuyos***	**los suyos**
	f.	**las mías**	**las tuyas***	**las suyas**
possessor more than one person	singular m.	**el nuestro**	**el vuestro***	**el suyo**
	f.	**la nuestra**	**la vuestra***	**la suya**
	plural m.	**los nuestros**	**los vuestros***	**los suyos**
	f.	**las nuestras**	**las vuestras***	**las suyas**

*cf. 12.2.5 for regional usage.

■ **12.3.2** The neuter article **lo** + the possessive can be used as a neuter construction: **lo mío** (*mine*), **lo nuestro** (*ours*), etc.

12.4 Meaning and Use of Pronouns

■ **12.4.1** The possessive pronouns mean the following:

el mío, los míos	*mine*
el tuyo, los tuyos	*yours*
el suyo, los suyos	*his/hers, yours, theirs*
el nuestro, los nuestros	*ours*
el vuestro, los vuestros	*yours (Spain only)*

Este bolso es **el mío, el tuyo** es el rojo.

*This bag is **mine; yours** is the red one.*

| Esta habitación no es **la nuestra**. | *This room is not **ours**.* |

■ 12.4.2 The Ambiguity of Possessive Pronouns

a The masculine and feminine forms and also the singular and plural forms refer to the possessed object and not the person who possesses it. It is therefore only the context that can determine who is the owner:

| Esta cartera es **suya** (de Ana/de Juan). | *This wallet is **his/hers** (Ana's/Juan's).* |

b In the case of the third person **suyo/a/os/as** it is often difficult to know whether the owner is one person or more than one, as these forms can refer to many different possessors—*his/hers/theirs/yours*:

| ¿Estas maletas son **suyas**? | *Are these suitcases **theirs/ yours/his/hers**?* |

c However, if the context does not make it clear, the ambiguity with regard to ownership can be clarified by using the **de** + personal pronoun construction at the end of the sentence: **de** + **él/ella, ellos/ellas, ustedes**:

| ¿Estas maletas son **de él**? | *Are these suitcases **his**?* |

■ 12.4.3 The possessive pronoun is not used when there is already a personal pronoun in the sentence:

| **Me** lavo **las** manos. | *I wash **my** hands.* |
| **Se** puso **el** abrigo. | *She put **her** coat on.* |

■ 12.4.4 If the pronoun is preceded by the plural article, it means *their own kind, family*:

| María pasa las vacaciones con **los suyos**. | *María is spending her vacation with **her family**.* |

■ **12.4.5** Possessive pronouns are usually preceded by the article:

Tu habitación es mejor que la mía.　　*Your room is better than **mine**.*

■ **12.4.6** After the verb **ser** (*to be*) the article can be omitted:

Este libro es **mío**.　　*This book is **mine**.*

■ **12.4.7** But it has a different meaning, and expresses more emphasis, if the article is used:

Este libro es **el mío**.　　*This book is **mine** (as opposed to anyone else's).*

■ **12.4.8** Possessive pronouns can act as nouns if used with the article **lo**:

Esto es **lo mío**.　　*This is my stuff (these are my things).*

■ **12.4.9** Cuyo (*whose*) is a relative pronoun with a possessive meaning:

La chica **cuya** carta recibí ayer se llama Carmen.　　*The girl **whose** letter I received yesterday is called Carmen.*

For more explanation of **cuyo** see 13.6 on relative pronouns.

13 Relative Pronouns

Relative pronouns refer to a noun or an action earlier in the sentence. These are called the antecedents.

Los chicos **que** estudian español irán a España. Los otros no.	*The boys (who are) studying Spanish will go to Spain. The others won't.*

13.1 Form

The relative forms are **que** (*that, who*), **cual, cuales** (*which*), **quien, quienes** (*who*), and **cuyo, cuya, cuyos, cuyas** (*whose*).

Unlike English equivalents, relative pronouns cannot be omitted.

masculine	feminine	masculine plural	feminine plural
que (invariable)			
cual		**cuales**	
quien		**quienes**	
cuyo	**cuya**	**cuyos**	**cuyas**

■ **13.1.1** Que is invariable. **Cual** and **quien** only change in number: to **cuales** and **quienes**. **Cuyo** changes in gender and number to **cuya, cuyos, cuyas**.

■ **13.1.2** Que is often accompanied by the article in order to be more specific in its agreement with the antecedent. **Cual** must always be accompanied by an article:

masculine	feminine	masculine plural	feminine plural
el que	**la que**	**los que**	**las que**
el cual	**la cual**	**los cuales**	**las cuales**

13.2 *Que*

■ **13.2.1** The most commonly used relative pronoun is **que**. It is used for both people and things and it means *who, whom, which, that*:

Este es el médico **que** trabaja en el hospital.	*This is the doctor **who** works in the hospital.*
La película **que** vamos a ver es muy buena.	*The film (that) we are going to see is very good.*

■ **13.2.2** **Que** can be used on its own:

Luis es el chico **que** encontramos ayer.	*Luis is the boy (**whom**) I met yesterday.*

■ **13.2.3** It can be preceded by a preposition. In this case **que** is often accompanied by the article: **el que**, **la que**, **los que**, **las que**:

Luis es el chico **al que** encontramos ayer.	*Luis is the boy (**whom**) I met yesterday.*

■ **13.2.4** **Que** accompanied by a preposition can also be used in some cases without the article, except when the preposition has two or more syllables:

El avión **en que** viajamos es muy cómodo.	*The plane we are traveling in is very comfortable.*
El equipo **contra el que** jugaremos es muy malo.	*The team against which we'll play is very bad.*

13.3 *Quien*

Quien is only used when referring to people and can be a substitute for **que**. It is more formal and literary and a lot less common than **que**, especially in spoken Spanish.

Vino con sus padres, **quienes** llegaron muy cansados.	*He came with his parents, **who** arrived very tired.*

It is used more with prepositions:

Éste es el hombre **con**
quien tienes que hablar.

*This is the man **with whom** you*
have to speak.

13.4 *Cual*

Cual can substitute **que** whether it refers to a person or an object. There is no difference in meaning with **que**, but **el cual** is used mainly in literary texts and very formal language.
It is only used preceded by an article:

El profesor, **el cual** dio la
clase ayer, es excelente.

*The teacher **who** gave the*
lesson yesterday is excellent.

It is also used more if accompanied by a preposition:

El escritor **al cual** darán
un homenaje nació en
México.

*The writer **to whom** they will*
pay the homage was born in
Mexico.

13.5 *Que, Quien, el Cual*

Of all these forms **que** is the one used most often and is also the simplest.
Compare:

Que:	El chico **que** conocí ayer es muy simpático.	
Al que:	El chico **al que** conocí ayer es muy simpático.	*The boy whom I met yesterday is very nice.*
A quien:	El chico **a quien** conocí ayer es muy simpático.	
Al cual:	El chico **al cual** conocí ayer es muy simpático.	

13.6 *Cuyo, Cuya, Cuyos, Cuyas*

This relative pronoun means *whose* and is only used to express possession. It is the equivalent of **de quien**, **del**

que, del cual.

Cuyo agrees in number and gender with the noun that follows it and is only used in literary and very formal language:

Una mujer **cuyo** nombre no recuerdo te ha llamado.	*A woman **whose** name I don't remember phoned you.*

13.7 The Neuter Form *Lo Que*

Lo que is used when the antecedent is a whole clause or a concept:

No entiendo **lo que** dices.	*I don't understand **what** you are saying.*
Lo que más me gusta de la película es la música.	***What** I like most about the film is the music.*

■ **13.7.1** **Lo que** can sometimes be substituted by the interrogative **qué**:

¿Me dices **lo que** has hecho hoy?	*Are you going to tell me what you did today?*
¿Me dices **qué** has hecho hoy?	*Are you going to tell me what you did today?*

■ **13.7.2** When the sentence starts with a relative pronoun that is a generalized form we can use **quien** or **el/la/los/las que** and in these cases they refer only to people:

Quien habla mejor español es Ana.	*The one who speaks the best Spanish is Ana.*
Los que llegan tarde no pueden entrar.	*Those who arrive late cannot enter.*

See section 17.8 for relative adverbs.

14.1 Form

Their form is the same as that of the relative pronouns but the interrogative pronouns have accents.

The interrogative pronouns are:

masculine		feminine		neuter
singular	plural	singular	plural	
qué		qué		qué
quién	quiénes	quién	quiénes	
cuál	cuáles	cuál	cuáles	
cuánto	cuántos	cuánta	cuántas	cuánto

14.2 ¿Quién, Quiénes?

These are only used when referring to persons. They mean *who?* and *whom?* or, with prepositions, *whose?*

¿**Quién** es?	*Who is it?*
¿**Quién** es el nuevo profesor?	*Who is the new teacher?*
¿De **quién** es este libro?	*Whose is this book?*

14.3 ¿Qué?

It means *what?* and is invariable in number and gender.
It can be used as a pronoun:

| ¿**Qué** has comprado? | *What have you bought?* |

and as an adjective:

| ¿**Qué** coche vas a comprar? | *Which car are you going to buy?* |

¿**Qué**? (*Pardon?*) is used to ask for a repetition; it is less formal than ¿**cómo**?:

| ¿**Qué** dices? | *What did you say?* |

14.4 ¿Cuál, Cuáles?

It means *which?* or *which one?, which ones?* It has the same form for the masculine and the feminine. It is appropriate in cases of choice:

¿**Cuál** te gusta más, el abrigo rojo o el azul?	*Which do you like more, the red overcoat or the blue one?*
¿**Cuáles** son tus cuadernos?	*Which are your exercise books?*

Cuál is not used as an adjective.

14.5 Difference Between ¿Qué? and ¿Cuál?

The main difference between ¿**qué?** and ¿**cuál?** is that ¿**qué?** can be followed by a noun and a verb, but ¿**cuál?** can only be followed by a verb (usually *to be* or *prefer*) or the preposition **de** followed by a pronoun or a noun:

¿**Qué** animal prefieres?	*Which animal do you prefer?*
¿**Cuál** es tu animal favorito?	*Which is your favorite animal?*
¿**Cuál** de los dos te gusta más?	*Which of the two do you like more?*
¿**Cuáles** prefieres?	*Which ones do you prefer?*

■ **14.5.1** Both ¿**qué?** and ¿**cuál?** can be followed by a verb. In this case ¿**qué?** asks for the essence, the type, or the nature or species of something and ¿**cuál?** asks for an individuality, establishing an option or choice:

¿**Qué** te gusta comer?	*What do you like to eat?*
¿**Cuál** es tu plato preferido, la carne o el pescado?	*Which is your favorite dish, meat, or fish?*

■ **14.5.2** ¿**Cuál?** is used with **éste** and **ésta** but it is never used with **esto**:

¿**Cuál** es éste?	*Which one is this?*

■ **14.5.3** ¿Qué? is used with **esto** but not with **éste** or **ésta**:

    ¿**Qué** es esto?   *What's that?*

14.6 ¿Cuánto?

■ **14.6.1** ¿Cuánto? can function as a pronoun or an adjective. It changes in gender (¿**cuánta?**) and in number (¿**cuántos?**, ¿**cuántas?**):

    ¿**Cuánta** carne quiere?   *How much meat would you like?*
    ¿**Cuántos** tomates quiere?   *How many tomatoes would you like?*

■ **14.6.2** ¿Cuánto? can also function as an adverb; in this case it is invariable. It means *how much?*:

    ¿**Cuánto** es?   *How much is it?*

14.7 ¿Cómo?

It means *how?*:

    ¿**Cómo** estás?   *How are you?*
    ¿**Cómo** viajarás?   *How will you travel?*

It is used to ask for repetition more formally than using ¿qué?:

    ¿**Cómo?**   *What?*

14.8 ¿Dónde?

It means *where?* and can be accompanied by different prepositions:

    ¿**Dónde** está la calle Mayor?   *Where is Main Street?*
    ¿Por **dónde** se va a la Plaza   *How do I/you get to the*
    Real?   *Royal Square?*

14.9 ¿Por qué?

It means *why?*:

    ¿**Por qué** no vamos al teatro   *Why don't we go to the*
    esta noche?   *theater tonight?*

14.10 ¿Para qué?

It means *what for?*:

¿**Para qué** has comprado esto?   *What have you bought this for?*

14.11 Indirect Questions

All these interrogative pronouns and adverbs can also be used in indirect questions. They do not have question marks but the interrogative pronouns and adverbs keep their accents:

No sé **dónde** he puesto las llaves.   *I don't know where I put the keys.*

Dime **cómo** lo quieres.   *Tell me how you would like it.*

14.12 Lo Que

Lo que meaning *what* can substitute interrogative **qué** in indirect sentences:

No sé **lo que/qué** voy a hacer.   *I don't know what I'm going to do.*

14.13 Exclamatory Pronouns and Adverbs

They have the same form as the interrogative pronouns and adverbs.

■ **14.13.1** ¡Qué! is invariable and is used in many idiomatic sentences:

¡**Qué** bonito!   *How pretty!*
¡**Qué** frío!   *It's so cold!*

■ **14.13.2** ¡Quién! varies in number (**quiénes**):

¡Mira **quiénes** son!   *Look who is here!*

■ **14.13.3** ¡Cuánto! varies in gender and it also varies in number:

¡**Cuánta** gente!	*What a lot of people!*
¡**Cuántos** niños estudian español!	*What a lot of children study Spanish!*

In the neuter, it means *a lot*.

¡**Cuánto** te quiero!	*I love you so much!*

■ **14.13.4** ¡Cómo! is invariable:

¡**Cómo** no!	*Of course!*

15 Indefinites

Indefinite adjectives and pronouns are used to talk about people or things without identifying them. They are words like **alguien** (*someone*), **nada** (*nothing*), **otro** (*other*). The forms of the majority of indefinite adjectives and pronouns are the same. Some can also act as adverbs.

15.1 The Indefinite Adjectives *Cada* and *Cierto*

■ **15.1.1** Cada means *each* or *every*. It does not change in number or gender:

Va al cine **cada** día.	*He goes to the movies every day.*

Cada also means *all sorts of* in familiar language:

Se ve **cada** vestido por aquí.	*You can see all kinds of dresses here.*

■ **15.1.2** Cierto can only be used as an adjective and it is variable in both gender and number (**cierto, cierta, ciertos, ciertas**):

Ciertos estudiantes no saben comportarse.	*Certain students don't know how to behave.*

If **cierto** is placed after a noun it means *true, accurate, fixed*:

Tenemos noticias **ciertas** de la situación.	*We have definite news about the situation.*

15.2 Indefinite Pronouns

The most frequently used are:

algo	*something*	refer to things or concepts.
nada	*nothing*	
alguien	*someone*	refer to people.
nadie	*no one*	

None of these forms vary in gender or number.

■ **15.2.1 Algo** means *something* and in questions *anything*:

Tengo **algo** para ti.	*I have something for you.*
¿Quiere **algo** más?	*Would you like anything else?*

■ **15.2.2 Nada** means *nothing* or *anything*:

No me queda **nada**.	*I have nothing left.*
No quiero **nada** más.	*I don't want anything else.*

■ **15.2.3 Alguien** means *someone/somebody* or *anyone/anybody*, and **nadie** means *nobody*:

¿Ha llamado **alguien**?	*Has anyone called?*
No, no ha llamado **nadie**.	*No, nobody has called.*

15.3 Indefinite Adjectives and Pronouns

Many indefinite words can be used both as adjectives and pronouns.

■ **15.3.1 Alguno/alguna/algunos/algunas:**

Vienen **algunos** amigos esta tarde. (adjective)	*Some of my friends are coming this afternoon.*
Hay muchos monumentos aquí. **Algunos** son romanos. (pronoun)	*There are a lot of monuments here. Some are Roman.*

Ninguno/ninguna:

No tiene **ningún** amigo. (adjective)	*He doesn't have any friends.*
Tiene amigos, pero no se entiende con **ninguno**. (pronoun)	*She has friends but she doesn't get on with any of them.*

■ **15.3.2** When used as adjectives, **alguno** is shortened to **algún** and **ninguno** to **ningún**:

¿Ha venido **algún** cliente? (adjective)	*Have any customers come?*

No ha venido **ninguno**.	No one has come.
(pronoun)	
No tiene **ningún** problema.	He doesn't have any problems.
(adjective)	

Alguno and **ninguno** are similar in use to **alguien** and **nadie**, respectively. The difference is that the first two may be used to specify someone particular in a group—**alguno de ellos** or **ninguno de ellos**:

¿Vino **alguien**?	Did anyone come?
¿Vino **alguno** (de ellos)?	Did any of them come?

■ 15.3.3 Uno/una/unos/unas:

¿Quieres **unos** bocadillos?	Do you want some
(adjective)	sandwiches?
No tengo bolígrafo. ¿Me	I don't have a pen. Can you
dejas **uno**? (pronoun)	lend me one?

For the impersonal use of **uno** see 34.4. For **uno** as a numeral see 16.2. For its use as an indefinite article see section 6.

■ 15.3.4 Otro/otra/otros/otras:

¿Quieres **otro** refresco?	Do you want another soft
(adjective)	drink?
No me gusta este vestido,	I don't like this dress, but I
pero no tengo **otro**.	don't have another one.
(pronoun)	

■ 15.3.5 Varios/varias (only in plural) means *several* or *various*:

Tiene **varios** sobrinos.	He has several nephews and
(adjective)	nieces.
Leo muchos periódicos;	I read a lot of newspapers;
todos los días compro	every day I buy several.
varios. (pronoun)	

■ **15.3.6 Cualquiera** used as an adjective means *any* and as a pronoun *anybody/anyone*.

As an adjective the final **a** of **cualquiera** is dropped and becomes **cualquier**:

Puedes tomar **cualquier** tren. (adjective)   *You can take any train.*

Puedes usar **cualquier** taza.   *You can use any cup.*

Cualquiera usually precedes the noun but it can be placed after the noun to emphasize the randomness of choice:

Dame una revista **cualquiera**. *Give me any magazine.*

15.4 Indefinites as Adverbs

■ **15.4.1** The following can be adverbs as well as adjectives and pronouns:

todo	mucho	poco	demasiado

As adjectives and pronouns, these change in gender and number. As adverbs they are invariable and do not change:

Me gusta **todo**.   *I like everything.*

Me gusta **mucho** el café.   *I like coffee very much.*

Esta música me gusta **poco**.   *I don't like this music very much.*

Habla **demasiado**.   *He talks too much.*

■ **15.4.2 Algo** and **nada** as neuters can also act as adverbs, **algo** meaning *rather* or *a bit*, and **nada** meaning *not at all*:

La película es **algo** aburrida.   *The film is a bit boring.*

No es **nada** interesante.   *It isn't at all interesting.*

For **nada** and **nadie** see section 18 on negatives.

■ **15.4.3 Bastante** as an adjective often means *a lot*. As an adverb it means *a lot* and *enough*:

| Tiene **bastantes** clientes. | *He has quite a lot of customers.* |
| ¿Ha comido usted **bastante**? | *Have you eaten enough?* |

■ **15.4.4** Tanto/tanta/tantos/tantas is an adjective variable in number and gender and it means *so much* or *so many*:
No puedo comer **tanta** paella. *I can't eat so much paella.*

a As an adverb it is invariable and the neuter **tanto** is used:
No puedo andar **tanto**.   *I can't walk so much.*

b There are a few idiomatic expressions with **tanto** that are very common in Spanish:
¡No es para **tanto**!   *Don't exaggerate!*
¡No **tanto**!   *Not so much!*

The shorter form of **tanto**, **tan** is required before adjectives or adverbs:
¡Se despierta **tan** temprano!   *He wakes up so early!*

For uses of **tan** and **tanto** in comparisons see section 8.

16 Numerals

Numerals are divided into cardinal and ordinal numbers.

16.1 Form of Cardinal Numbers

0 cero	11 once	21 veintiuno/a
1 uno/una	12 doce	22 veintidós
2 dos	13 trece	23 veintitrés
3 tres	14 catorce	24 veinticuatro
4 cuatro	15 quince	25 veinticinco
5 cinco	16 dieciséis	26 veintiséis
6 seis	17 diecisiete	27 veintisiete
7 siete	18 dieciocho	28 veintiocho
8 ocho	19 diecinueve	29 veintinueve
9 nueve	20 veinte	30 treinta
10 diez		

■ **16.1.1** Note that from sixteen to thirty the numbers are contracted into one word. From thirty on the numbers are separated and linked by **y** (*and*):

31 treinta y uno	40 cuarenta	60 sesenta
32 treinta y dos	45 cuarenta y cinco	67 sesenta y siete
33 treinta y tres	50 cincuenta	70 setenta
34 treinta y cuatro	56 cincuenta y seis	78 setenta y ocho

80 ochenta	101 ciento uno/a
89 ochenta y nueve	105 ciento cinco
90 noventa	111 ciento once
100 cien, ciento	125 ciento veinticinco
	186 ciento ochenta y seis

■ **16.1.2** Note that **cien** is the shortened form of **ciento**. It is used to signify 100. If other numbers follow, **ciento** must be used.

El pueblo tiene **cien** habitantes.	*The village has one hundred inhabitants.*
El bolígrafo cuesta **ciento cincuenta** pesos.	*The pen costs 150 pesos.*

■ **16.1.3** **Ciento** is kept in expressions of percentages:
el veinticinco por **ciento** de descuento   *25 percent discount*

■ **16.1.4** Numbers are masculine (**el dos, el tres**) except for **uno/una**. But from **doscientos** (200) through **novecientos** (900), numbers can be feminine or masculine depending on the noun they are accompanying or referring to:

doscientos francos	*200 francs*
doscientas pesos	*200 pesos*

They are as follows:

200	doscientos/doscientas	500	quinientos/as
235	doscientos/as treinta y cinco	600	seiscientos/as
300	trescientos/as	700	setecientos/as
350	trescientos/as cincuenta	800	ochocientos/as
400	cuatrocientos/as	900	novecientos/as

■ **16.1.5** From **mil** (one thousand) numbers are again invariable. A period is used to separate thousands, not a comma as in English: 2.000 (**dos mil**), 3.000 (**tres mil**), etc.

16.2 Use of Cardinal Numbers

■ **16.2.1** Un, Uno, Una

Uno has a feminine form **una**. If **uno** precedes a noun it is shortened to **un**. Also **veintiuno** gets shortened to **veintiún**.

Arturo tiene **un** niño y **una** niña.	*Arturo has one boy and one girl.*
Jaime tiene **veintiún** años.	*Jaime is twenty-one years old.*

■ **16.2.2** **Ciento** (*one hundred*) and **mil** (*one thousand*) are invariable—they do not change to the feminine or the plural. **Millón** (*a million*) changes only to the plural. It is always masculine.

ciento dos pesos	*102 pesos*
mil pesos	*1,000 pesos*
Ganó **dos millones** en la lotería.	*He won two million in the lottery.*

a   But when they act as nouns they can be used in the plural—**cientos**, *hundreds*; **miles**, *thousands*—and are followed by the preposition **de**:

Cientos de personas han visto este espectáculo.	*Hundreds of people have seen this show.*
Cada año **miles de** turistas visitan España.	*Each year thousands of tourists visit Spain.*

b   Also **un millón** (*one million*), **dos millones** (*two million*), etc., are followed by **de** if they precede a noun:

Ganó diez **millones de** pesos en la lotería.	*He won ten million pesos in the lottery.*

■ **16.2.3** Centuries are expressed by cardinal numbers:

el siglo **veinte**	*the twentieth century*

■ **16.2.4** **Ambos** means **los dos** (*both*) and it is always plural, but it changes according to gender—**ambas**:

Compra **ambos** cuadros.	*Buy both paintings.*
Me gustan **ambas** casas.	*I like both houses.*

16.3 Form of Ordinal Numbers

primero 1°	*first 1st*	sexto 6°	*sixth 6th*
segundo 2°	*second 2nd*	séptimo 7°	*seventh 7th*
tercero 3°	*third 3rd*	octavo 8°	*eighth 8th*
cuarto 4°	*fourth 4th*	noveno 9°	*ninth 9th*
quinto 5°	*fifth 5th*	décimo 10°	*tenth 10th*

The ordinal forms after 10 are hardly used and only in formal language.

16.4 Use of Ordinal Numbers

■ **16.4.1** In modern spoken and written Spanish the cardinal forms are used for ordinals after tenth:

el piso **catorce**   *the fourteenth floor*

Ordinal numbers vary according to gender and number:

Vivo en el **décimo** piso,   *I live on the tenth floor, second*
segunda puerta a la   *door to the left.*
izquierda.

17 Adverbs

Adverbs are words that modify and determine the verb, as in **conduce rápidamente** (*he drives fast*). They are complex and varied both in form and function. They can also modify and determine:

- adjectives: **muy bonito** (*very pretty*);

- other adverbs: **muy bien** (*very well*);

and accompany prepositions and conjunctions.

17.1 Form of Adverbs

There are two general forms for adverbs.

■ **17.1.1** Invariable adverbs that do not change in number or gender: **bien** (*well*), **mal** (*bad* or *badly*), **lejos** (*far* or *a long way*), **ayer** (*yesterday*).

■ **17.1.2** Adverbs ending in -**mente**
They are those that add -**mente** to the feminine form of the adjective: **espontáneamente**, (*spontaneously*), **tranquilamente** (*quietly*).
Not all adjectives take -**mente**. Those that do can be described as adverbs of manner:

lenta	→	**mente** (*slowly*)
tranquila	→	**mente** (*quietly*)

Trabaja muy **lentamente**.   *He works very slowly.*

■ **17.1.3** When there are two or more adverbs in a sentence where the ending would normally be -**mente**, only the last carries the ending -**mente**:

Me gusta pasear **tranquila**   *I like to walk quietly and slowly*
y lentamente por la playa.   *along the beach.*

■ **17.1.4** Adverbs ending in -**mente** keep their normal stress/accent. As -**mente** is a stressed form some adverbs have a stress syllable in addition to -**mente**:

Hace los deberes **fácilmente**. *She does her homework easily.*

■ **17.1.5** There are some adjectives that cannot take -**mente**:

a   Adjectives indicating physical appearance: **gordo** (*fat*), **viejo** (*old*).

b   Colors: **rojo** (*red*), **amarillo** (*yellow*).

c   Nationalities and origin: **español**, **neoyorquino**.

d   Ordinal numbers: **tercero** (*third*), **quinto** (*fifth*).

Note the exceptions: **primeramente** (*firstly*) and **últimamente** (*lastly*).

17.2 Position of Adverbs

Most adverbs usually follow the verb:

María habla **bien** el español. *María speaks Spanish well.*

■ **17.2.1** The adverbs **sí**, **no**, **sólo**, and **casi** usually precede the verb:

No come mucho. *He doesn't eat much.*
Casi tenemos un accidente. *We almost had an accident.*

17.3 Adverbs of Manner

They are words that express the way something is done. These are some of the most common ones: **deprisa** (*quickly*), **aprisa** (*quickly*), **despacio** (*slowly*), **pronto** (*soon*), **bien** (*well*), **mal** (*bad, badly*), **así** (*like this*).

Many of those ending in -**mente** are adverbs of manner: **lentamente** (*slowly*), **fácilmente** (*easily*).

17.4 Adverbs of Place or Position

These are some of the most common ones: **aquí, acá** (*here*), **ahí, allí, allá** (*there*), **delante** (*in front*), **detrás** (*behind*), **debajo** (*below, under*), **cerca** (*near*), **lejos** (*a long way*).

■ **17.4.1** The use of **aquí** (*here*) and **ahí, allí** (*there*) depends on the distance of the person or object mentioned in relation to the speaker. They are related to **éste** (*this*), **ése** (*that*), and **aquél** (*that*).

Usted puede sentarse **aquí** y el señor **ahí**, al otro lado.	*You can sit here and the gentleman there, on the other side.*
El hotel está **allí**, un poco lejos.	*The hotel is there, quite a long way away.*

17.5 Adverbs of Time

Here are some of the most common ones: **ahora** (*now*), **ayer** (*yesterday*), **hoy** (*today*), **mañana** (*tomorrow*), **tarde** (*late*), **pronto** (*early* or *soon*).

For **nunca** and **jamás** see section 18 on negatives.

■ **17.5.1** **Ya** (*already*) can be an adverb and also can act as a linking word, or conjunction.

a Adverb:
   El avión **ya** ha llegado.   *The plane has just/already arrived.*

b Conjunction:
   Ya haga sol, **ya** llueva saldremos.   *Whether it is sunny or it rains, we'll go out.*

■ **17.5.2** **Ya** has many idiomatic uses. It is used to express affirmation, impatience, certainty, or resignation:

a Affirmation:
¿Lo comprendes?   *Do you understand? Yes, of*
¡**Ya**, claro!   *course!*

b Impatience:
¡**Ya** voy!   *I'm coming now!*

c Certainty:
Ya habrán terminado.   *They will have finished already.*

d Resignation:
Ya verás.   *You'll see.*

e The following are useful examples of **ya**:
Ya lo sé.   *Yes, I know that.*
¡Entra **ya**!   *Go in now!*
¡Basta **ya**!   *That's enough now!*

■ **17.5.3 Aún** and **todavía** (*yet*)—these two words mean
the same and are interchangeable:
El autobús **aún** no ha llegado. *The bus hasn't arrived yet.*
El tren **todavía** no ha llegado. *The train hasn't arrived yet.*

Aun without an accent means *even*:
Aun comiendo mucho   *Even though she eats a lot she*
no engorda.   *doesn't get fat.*

■ **17.5.4** There is a difference between **ya no** and **aún no**.

a **Ya no** means that something that used to take place no
longer does so:
Ya no trabaja en aquel   *He's no longer working in that*
restaurante.   *restaurant.*

Or something you were expecting to happen will not
now happen:
Es tarde y **ya no** viene.   *It's late and he won't come*
                                 now.

b **Aún no** means that something has not taken place yet:
  Es tarde y **aún no** viene.   *It's late and he still hasn't come.*

17.6 Adverbs of Quantity

Some of the most common ones are: **mucho** (*a lot*), **muy**
(*very*), **poco** (*little*), **algo** (*some*), **nada** (*nothing*), **demasiado**
(*too much, too many*), **más** (*more*).

■ **17.6.1** **Muy** and **mucho**—both these words have the
same meaning. But **muy** is used before adjectives:
  Es **muy** bonito.   *It's very pretty.*

and **mucho** goes before or after the verb:
  Llueve **mucho**.   *It's raining a lot.*

■ **17.6.2** **Más** means *more* or *best* and **menos** means *less*:
  ¿Cuál te gusta **más**?   *Which one do you like best?*
  ¿Cuál cuesta **menos**?   *Which one costs less?*

■ **17.6.3** **Tan** and **tanto** are used in exclamations:
  ¡Lo hizo **tan** rápidamente!   *He did it so quickly!*
  ¡Me gusta **tanto**!   *I like it so much!*

■ **17.6.4** **Más**, **menos**, **tan**, and **tanto** indicate
comparison (see section 8). Note that **más** and **menos** take
de or **que**:
  Estudia **más que** antes.   *He studies more than before.*
  Tiene **menos de** lo que   *He has less than he thinks.*
  piensa.

17.7 Affirmative and Negative Adverbs

Affirmative adverbs express affirmative moods and are
used for emphasis in a sentence:
  ¿Le gusta la comida?   *Do you like the meal?*
  Sí, me gusta mucho.   *Yes, it's lovely.*

Some of the most common ones are: **sí** (*yes*), **seguramente** (*certainly*), **también** (*also*), **claro** (*of course*).
Note that sí can be followed by **que** to add emphasis:

    Sí que ha llegado.   *Yes, of course he has arrived.*

■ **17.7.1** Negative adverbs are used to show adverbs in the negative mood. They are: **no**, **ni**, **jamás**, **tampoco**.
For use of negative adverbs see section 18 on negatives.

17.8 Relative Adverbs

Donde (*where*), **cuando** (*when*), **cuanto** (*how much, many*), and **como** (*as/like*) without accent are called relative adverbs:

    La casa **donde** vive Luis es   *The house where Luis lives is*
    muy grande.   *very big.*

17.9 Interrogative Adverbs

Dónde, **cuándo**, **cuánto**, and **cómo** with the accent are interrogative adverbs (see interrogative pronouns in section 14):

    ¿**Dónde** vive Luis?   *Where does Luis live?*

17.10 Comparison of Adverbs

Adverbs can be used for comparison and to express the superlative. These work in a similar way to the comparison of adjectives:

    En Estados Unidos se come   *In the United States mealtimes*
    más temprano **que** en   *are earlier than in Mexico.*
    México.
    Habla español **tan** bien   *She speaks Spanish as well*
    como tú.   *as you.*

-ísimo/a, **-ísimos/as** can be added to some adverbs to form the superlative: **prontísimo** (*very soon*), **muchísimo** (*very much*), **tantísimo** (*so much*), **cerquísima** (*very near*).

18 Negation

In Spanish there are various ways of expressing negation. The most common Spanish negative words are:

no	*no*	nada	*nothing*
ni	*nor*	nadie	*nobody*
jamás	*never*	ninguno	*none, nobody*
nunca	*never*	tampoco	*not either*

There are also a number of adverbial negative expressions. Here are some of them: **de ninguna manera** (*no way*), **de ningún modo** (*no way*), **claro que no** (*of course not*), **nada más** (*no more*).

18.1 *No*

■ **18.1.1** No normally precedes the word that it negates:

No tengo hermanos.　　　*I don't have any brothers or sisters.*

However, when there are object personal pronouns in the sentence before the verb, **no** is placed before them:

No se lo daré.　　　*I won't give it to him/her.*

■ **18.1.2** ¿No? at the end of a sentence is not a negative but a question tag. It means *isn't it? aren't you? don't you?*, etc. The speaker already knows the answer:

Volverás tarde, **¿no?**　　　*You'll be coming back late, won't you?*

■ **18.1.3** No más is another tag used in Latin American Spanish with different meanings—*just, only*, or used for emphasis:

Está en esta calle **no más**.　　　*It is just on this street.*

Llegó ayer **no más**.　　　*He arrived only yesterday.*

18.2 Double Negatives

■ **18.2.1** If a negative follows a verb, in Spanish there must always be another negative preceding the verb:

No quiero **nada** más, gracias. — *I don't want anything else thanks.*

■ **18.2.2** No is also used to reinforce other negative adverbs in certain cases:

No . . . nada:
No me gusta **nada**. — *I don't like it at all.*
No . . . nunca:
No me llama **nunca**. — *She never ever phones me.*
No . . . tampoco:
No me ha invitado **tampoco**. — *She hasn't invited me either.*

■ **18.2.3** It is also possible to start the sentence with other negatives:

Nunca come **nada**. — *She never eats anything.*
Nadie viene **nunca** a este sitio. — *Nobody ever comes to this place.*

■ **18.2.4** It is important to remember that when negatives other than **no** are placed before the verb it is not necessary to have another negative after the verb:

Nunca me llama. — *He never calls me.*
Tampoco me ha invitado a mí. — *He hasn't invited me either.*

18.3 *Ni*

In a negative sentence where there is only a single subject but two verbs, two negatives must be used. Generally, the first negative is **no** and comes before the first verb. The second negative, **ni**, comes before the second verb.

Sometimes the negative before the first verb is also **ni**:

No le gusta el cine **ni** le gusta la televisión.	*He doesn't like the cinema nor television.*
Ni va de vacaciones **ni** sale de casa los domingos.	*She neither goes on vacation nor goes out on Sundays.*

18.4 *Nada*

Nada generally means *nothing*:

Nada le gusta.	*Nothing pleases him.*

■ **18.4.1** **Nada** can act as an intensifier:

Este vino no me gusta **nada**.	*I don't like this wine at all.*

18.5 *Nadie*

If **nadie** (*nobody*) is the object of the verb, it is preceded by the preposition **a**:

No he visto **a nadie** por aquí.	*I haven't seen anyone around here.*

18.6 *Ninguno*

Ninguno can be a pronoun or an adjective. It changes gender by adding **-a** (feminine form: **ninguna**). When it is an adjective preceding a noun, **ninguno** loses the final **-o** and becomes **ningún**:

No tiene **ningún** amigo.	*She hasn't got any friends.*

See section 15 on indefinites.

18.7 *Nunca* and *Jamás*

Both mean *never* and sometimes *ever* and can be used in double negations as seen above. **Jamás** has a stronger meaning than **nunca**, but it is used less.

Nunca/jamás tiene dinero.	*He never has any money.*
No va **nunca/jamás** a la playa de vacaciones.	*He never goes to the beach on vacation.*

18.8 *Tampoco*

Tampoco (*not either*) is the opposite of **también** (also). It requires a double negative construction if it follows the verb but not if it goes before:

El pescado **no** me gusta **tampoco**.	*I don't like fish either.*
Tampoco me gusta la carne.	*I don't like meat either.*

19 Prepositions

Prepositions are link words. They are used to relate words within a sentence. They are words like **con** (*with*), **en** (*in*), **de** (*of*), etc.

Vamos **a** la piscina **con** los niños.	*We are going **to** the swimming pool **with** the children.*

The prepositions are:
a, ante, bajo, con, contra, de, desde, durante, en, entre, hacia, hasta, para, por, según, sin, sobre, tras.

The following words are also considered as prepositions: **excepto** (*except*), **salvo** (*except*), **mediante** (*by means of*), **obstante** (usually preceded by **no**, meaning *nevertheless*).

19.1 *A*

The preposition **a** is very common. It is used in a variety of situations and can change meaning according to context:

■ **19.1.1** Indicating direction (going somewhere). It means *to, on, down, up, in*:

Voy **a** Guadalajara.	*I'm going **to** Guadalajara.*
Bajó **a** la calle.	*She went down **to** the street.*

■ **19.1.2** Expressions of time, meaning *at, until*, or *to*:

El avión sale **a** las ocho.	*The plane leaves **at** eight.*
Trabajo de las ocho **a** las tres.	*I work from eight **to** three.*

■ **19.1.3** With days and dates:

Estamos **a** jueves.	*It's Thursday.*

It is used in expressions such as: **a la mañana siguiente, al día siguiente**:

Juan llegó **a** la mañana siguiente.	*Juan arrived the next morning.*

■ 19.1.4 Expressing purpose:

Invité a María **a** cenar.   *I invited María to supper.*

■ 19.1.5 Place:

sentarse **a** la mesa	*to sit at the table*
a la sombra	*in the shade*
a la izquierda	*to the left*

■ 19.1.6 Describing the instrument for or means or manner of doing something:

escribir **a** máquina o **a** mano	*to write with a typewriter or by hand*
Voy **a** pie.	*I'm going on foot.*

Note: ir **en** bicicleta, *to go by bicycle*; ir **en** coche, *to go by car*.

■ 19.1.7 Specifying price:

Las naranjas están **a** cien pesos el kilo.   *Oranges are selling at 100 pesos a kilo.*

■ 19.1.8 Distribution:

Toca **a** cinco caramelos por niño.   *There are five candies per child.*

■ 19.1.9 Distance or speed:

La playa está **a** cinco kilómetros.	*The beach is five kilometers (about 3 miles) away.*
El coche va **a** cien kilómetros por hora.	*The car is going at 100 kilometers (62 miles) an hour.*

■ 19.1.10 Uses of **a** in grammatical constructions:

a It is used when the direct object of the sentence is a person:

Invité **a** María.   *I invited María.*

with the exception of expressions using **tener**, such as:

Tengo dos hijos.	*I have two children.*

b It is placed before the indirect object:

Dio la carta **a** María.	*He gave the letter to María.*
Se dedica **a** la pintura.	*He devotes himself to painting.*

c It is the equivalent of *when* in the construction
a + **el** + infinitive:

Al terminar el trabajo volveré a casa.	***When** I finish work I'll go home.*

19.2 *Con*

■ **19.2.1** **Con** means *with* (to be in the company of someone or together with something):

Voy al cine **con** mi amigo.	*I'm going to the movie with my friend.*

■ **19.2.2** It is used with instruments or tools:

Corta el pan **con** un cuchillo.	*He cuts the bread with a knife.*

■ **19.2.3** Expressing manner:

Hay que servir a los clientes **con** amabilidad.	*The customers should be served in a friendly manner.*

■ **19.2.4** Other expressions:

soñar **con**	*to dream about*
ser bueno/amable **con** alguien	*to be friendly toward someone*

19.3 *De*

■ **19.3.1** *From* (origin):

¿**De** dónde eres? Soy **de** Caracas.	*Where are you from? I'm from Caracas.*

■ **19.3.2** *From* (distance):

Hay veinte kilómetros **del** aeropuerto al hotel.	*The airport is twenty kilometers (12 miles) from the hotel.*

■ **19.3.3** *From* (time):

Trabaja **de** las nueve a las dos.	*He works from nine to two.*

■ **19.3.4** *When* or *during* (time):

Trabaja **de** día.	*He works during the day.*
Se marchó **de** mañana.	*She left early in the morning.*

■ **19.3.5** Expressing what something is made of:

Este vaso es **de** plástico.	*This glass is made of plastic.*
tortilla **de** patata	*potato omelette*

■ **19.3.6** Quality, description:

Es **de** color verde.	*It's green.*

■ **19.3.7** Possession:

El bolso es **de** mi amiga.	*The bag is my friend's.*
el padre **de** mi madre	*my mother's father*

■ **19.3.8** *About* with verbs such as **hablar** (*to speak* or *talk*), **quejarse** (*to complain*):

Luis se queja **de** todo.	*Luis complains about everything.*

■ **19.3.9** Purpose, what something is used for:

máquina **de** escribir	*typewriter*
bicicleta **de** montaña	*mountain bike*

For more uses of **de** see comparatives and superlatives in section 8.

19.4 *Desde*

■ **19.4.1** *From, since,* and *for* in expressions of time:

El vuelo es **desde** las cuatro hasta las siete.	*The flight lasts **from** four to seven o'clock.*
Te espero **desde** las once.	*I've been waiting for you **since** eleven o'clock.*
Vivo aquí **desde** hace dos años.	*I've been living here **for** two years.*

■ **19.4.2** Place:

El tren va a **desde** Madrid a Sevilla en tres horas.	*The train goes from Madrid to Seville in three hours.*

19.5 *En*

■ **19.5.1** Indicating time and place:

Iré de vacaciones **en** agosto.	*I'll go on vacation in August.*
Haré esto **en** cinco minutos.	*I'll do this in five minutes.*
Marta está **en** Perú de vacaciones.	*Marta is in Peru on vacation.*

■ **19.5.2** **En** can be used variously to convey position without being specific. It can mean *on, inside, at, into,* etc:

El libro está **en** el cajón.	*The book is **in** the drawer.*
El libro está **en** la mesa.	*The book is **on** the table.*
El chico está **en** el colegio.	*The boy is **at** school.*

■ **19.5.3** Transport:

viajar **en** avión	*to travel by plane*

■ **19.5.4** To speak a language:

hablar **en** español	*to speak in Spanish*

19.6 *Hacia*

■ **19.6.1** *Toward:*
Este autobús va **hacia** Puebla.   *This bus is going to Puebla.*

■ **19.6.2** *Around, about,* or *approximately* (in time):
Fernando llegará **hacia** las   *Fernando will arrive at about*
diez de la mañana.   *ten o'clock in the morning.*

19.7 *Hasta*

Used to express a limit in time or space (*until* and *as far as*):

Durmió **hasta** las seis.   *He slept until six.*
Hasta Barcelona hay   *There are two hundred*
doscientos kilómetros.   *kilometers (136 miles) to*
                                     Barcelona.

19.8 *Por*

■ **19.8.1** *For, because of.* Generally **por** expresses the cause of or reason for an action:

Este lugar es famoso **por**   *This place is famous for its*
sus playas.   *beaches.*
La carretera está cortada   *The road is closed because of*
por la nieve.   *the snow.*

■ **19.8.2** It forms part of ¿**por qué**? (*why?*) and **porque** (*because*):

¿**Por qué** llegas tarde?   *Why have you arrived late?*
Porque he perdido el tren.   *Because I missed the train.*

■ **19.8.3** *In* or *for* (approximate time or duration):
Vendrá **por** la mañana.   *She'll come in the morning.*
Vamos de vacaciones   *We are going on vacation for*
por un mes.   *a month.*

■ **19.8.4** *Through* (in the sense of place):

Todos los días paso **por** el parque para ir a casa.   *Every day I go through the park to get home.*

Entró **por** la ventana.   *He got in through the window.*

■ **19.8.5** *Around* (in a vague sense):

Paseaba **por** la ciudad.   *I walked around the city.*

La catedral está **por** aquí.   *The cathedral is around here.*

■ **19.8.6** *Along*

Siga **por** esa calle todo recto.   *Go straight along this street.*

■ **19.8.7** In expressions of movement, such as **por debajo** (*under*), **por encima** (*over*), **por delante de** (*in front of*), **por detrás de** (*behind*).

■ **19.8.8** It indicates the means of doing something:

Antes de mandarnos el documento **por** fax, llama **por** teléfono.   *Before you send us the document by fax, telephone me.*

■ **19.8.9** Rate and price:

Pagó cinco mil pesetas **por** esta falda.   *She paid five thousand pesetas for this skirt.*

■ **19.8.10** Expressing speed:

Está prohibido circular a más de cien kilómetros **por** hora.   *It's prohibited to drive at more than a hundred kilometers (62 miles) an hour.*

■ **19.8.11** Expressing equivalence:

Vale **por** una botella de champán.   *It's worth a bottle of champagne.*

■ **19.8.12** Distribution:

Pagamos setecientos pesos **por** persona.	*We paid seven hundred pesos per person.*

■ **19.8.13** *On behalf of*:

¿Puedo firmar **por** mi marido?	*Can I sign for my husband?*

■ **19.8.14** Expressing exchange:

¿Puedo cambiar este vestido **por** ese azul?	*Can I change this dress for that blue one?*

■ **19.8.15** It also means purpose. It can be confused with **para**, which also means *for*, and it is often interchangeable:

Trabajo **por** mi familia.	*I work for my family.*
Tengo muchas cosas **por** hacer.	*I have a lot of things to do.*

■ **19.8.16** It precedes the agent in passive constructions:

Este cuadro fue pintado **por** Goya.	*This picture was painted by Goya.*

See section 34 on the passive.

19.9 *Para*

■ **19.9.1** *For* or *in order to*. Generally **para** expresses intention, purpose, or destiny. In this case it can be confused with **por** as they both mean *for* in English:

Trabajo **para** comer.	*I work in order to eat.*
Estudio mucho **para** hablar bien el español.	*I'm studying a lot in order to speak Spanish well.*

■ **19.9.2** Direction and movement (toward somewhere):

El tren **para** Puebla saldrá a las tres.	*The train for Puebla will leave at three.*

■ **19.9.3** Approximate time:

¿Vendrás **para** el verano?   *Will you come for the summer?*

■ **19.9.4** The use of something:

Esto es muy bueno **para** la gripe.   *This is very good for the flu.*

Esto sirve **para** limpiar el baño.   *This can be used for cleaning the bathroom.*

■ **19.9.5** The proximity or starting of an action:

Está **para** llover.   *It's about to rain.*

■ **19.9.6** Accompanying the indirect object:

He comprado este regalo **para** Ana.   *I've bought this present for Ana.*

■ **19.9.7** With **mí** meaning *in my opinion*:

Para mí esto no está bien.   *As far as I'm concerned this isn't very good.*

■ **19.9.8** With **sí** in reflexive constructions meaning *to himself, herself,* or *themselves*:

dijo **para sí** . . .   *he said to himself . . .*

■ **19.9.9** In expressions of comparison, meaning *considering*:

Para ser principiante hablas español muy bien.   *For a beginner you speak Spanish very well.*

19.10 Other Prepositions

■ **19.10.1** Other prepositions such as **contra** (*against*), **durante** (*during*), **entre** (*between/among*), **según** (*according to*), and **sin** (*without*) correspond to their English equivalent. For example:

> **Durante** mi estancia en
> Francia visité Marsella.
> *During my time in France
> I visited Marseille.*
>
> Estoy **sin** trabajo.
> *I'm out of work.*

■ 19.10.2 *Sobre*

a *On* or *above* (in expressions of place):
> El reloj está **sobre** la cama.   *The watch is on the bed.*
> El avión vuela **sobre** el mar.   *The plane is flying over the sea.*

Note that **sobre** can be substituted by **en**, which has a more general meaning.

b It also means *about*:
> El profesor hablará hoy
> **sobre** las preposiciones.
> *The teacher will speak about
> prepositions today.*

c *Approximately*:
> El autobús llegará **sobre**
> las diez.
> *The bus will arrive at about ten.*

19.11 Prepositions as Prepositional Phrases

■ 19.11.1 *Ante*

a *In front of, in the presence of.* It is more often used in the form of a prepositional phrase **delante**, **delante de**:
> Cantó **ante** mucho
> público.
> *He sang in front of a
> huge audience.*
>
> El hotel está **delante de**
> la iglesia.
> *The hotel is in front of the
> church.*

b *Faced with* or *in the face of*:
> No sabe reaccionar **ante**
> un problema.
> *He doesn't know how to react to
> a problem.*

c **Ante todo** (*above all*):
   Me gusta **ante todo**   *I like to make new friends more*
   hacer nuevos amigos.   *than anything.*

■ 19.11.2 *Bajo*

a **Bajo**, also used more commonly as the prepositional
   phrase **debajo, debajo de,** means *under* or *underneath*:
   El barco pasa **bajo** el   *The boat passes under the*
   puente.   *bridge.*
   El gato está **debajo de**   *The cat is under the bed.*
   la cama.

b Also used in figurative terms:
   La economía no prospera   *The economy will not prosper*
   bajo este gobierno.   *under this government.*

■ 19.11.3 *Tras*

a *Behind* (expressing place):
   Se escondió **tras** la puerta. *He hid behind the door.*

   Note that it is more commonly used in combinations
   such as **detrás, detrás de**:
   La piscina está **detrás de**   *The swimming pool is behind*
   la casa.   *the house.*

b *After* (expressions of time):
   Tras la conferencia fueron   *After the conference they went*
   a comer.   *to eat.*

■ **19.11.4** Many prepositions combine with other words
to form prepositional phrases: **antes de** (*before*), **junto a**
(*alongside*), **al lado de** (*next to*), **encima de** (*on top of*),
enfrente de (*opposite*).

20 Conjunctions

Conjunctions are the words used to relate or link sentences or parts of sentences. They are words such as *and, or, nor, but*. They can link two separate, independent sentences or subordinate clauses.

20.1 *Y, E*

Y, e mean *and*; e has the same meaning as y but it is used when the following word starts with i or hi:

Compraré una postal y escribiré a Elena.	I'll buy a postcard **and** I'll write to Elena.
Teresa **e** Isabel llegarán mañana.	Teresa **and** Isabel are arriving tomorrow.

20.2 *Ni*

Ni is the negative form of y and it is repeated in the sentence. It means *neither . . . nor*:

Ni ha venido **ni** ha llamado para avisarnos.	He's **neither** arrived **nor** phoned to let us know.

20.3 *O, U*

O, u mean *or*; u is the same as o but it is used when the following word starts with o or ho:

¿Quieres café **o** té?	Would you like coffee **or** tea?
La niña tiene siete **u** ocho años.	The little girl is about seven **or** eight.

■ **20.3.1** It is used in the construction o . . . o with the meaning of *either . . . or*:

O entras **o** sales.	You **either** come in **or** go out.

20.4 *Pero, Sino, Mas*

Pero, sino, mas all mean *but*; mas is hardly used and shouldn't be confused with the adverb **más** (*more*):

| Quiero vino blanco **pero** muy frío. | *I'd like some white wine **but** very cold.* |

■ **20.4.1 Sino** differs from **pero** only in that it contradicts a preceding negative statement:

| No quiero vino blanco **sino** tinto. | *I don't want white wine; I want red.* |

20.5 *Que*

Que is used to link two sentences or clauses and introduces a subordinate clause. It means *that*. It is often followed by the subjunctive:

| En la carta dice **que** está bien. | *In the letter he says that he's well.* |
| Es mejor **que** llegues pronto. | *It's better that you come early.* |

20.6 *Porque*

Porque and, in some cases, **que** are used to link subordinate causal clauses:

| No puedo salir **porque** no tengo dinero. | *I can't go out **because** I don't have any money.* |
| No vayas **que** no quiere verte. | *Don't go **because** she doesn't want to see you.* |

20.7 *Pues*

Pues has a causal meaning:

| Voy a comprar este jarrón **pues** es muy bonito. | *I'm going to buy this jar **as** it is so pretty.* |

20.8 *Excepto, Menos, Salvo*

These mean *with the exception of*:

| Vinieron todos **excepto** los niños. | *They all came **except** the children.* |

21 Word Order

Word order in Spanish is very flexible, especially the position of the subject in relation to the verb. Clarity, style, and rhythm are important criteria. Usually the speaker tends to place what he or she perceives to be more important as the first element of the sentence. The most common construction in Spanish is to have the subject first and then the verb:

Luis viene.   *Luis is coming.*

It is possible to put the verb before the subject:

Viene Luis.   *Luis is coming.*

21.1 Questions

■ **21.1.1** In questions the verb is usually placed before the subject and this is followed by the object, if there is one:

¿Viene Ana con nosotros?   *Is Ana coming with us?*
¿Comprarás tú las entradas? *Will you buy the tickets?*

■ **21.1.2** But often intonation is enough to indicate the question, and the word order of the affirmative sentence is kept. This is the reason why the question mark is put upside down at the beginning of the sentence:

¿Ana viene con nosotros?   *Is Ana coming with us?*

21.2 Some Word Order Rules

In Spanish any part of the clause can be placed at the beginning of the sentence:

Hasta el día siguiente no   *Not until the following day did*
le entregaron la carta.   *they hand in the letter.*

■ **21.2.1** No words can be put between the auxiliary verb and the participle:

El autobús **ha salido** ya.   *The bus has left already.*

■ **21.2.2** Adverbs and adverbial phrases go immediately before or after the word they modify:

Luis **va frecuentemente**
a cenar al restaurante.

Luis goes to eat at the
restaurant frequently.

For word order with personal pronouns see section 9. For position of adjectives see section 7. For word order with negatives see section 18.

22 Verbs

Verbs are words like **hablar** (*to speak*), **comer** (*to eat*), and **vivir** (*to live*), which are concerned with what people and things do and what happens to them.

22.1 The Infinitive

The infinitive is the basic form found in the dictionary. In English the infinitive has the word *to* before it.
The infinitive expresses meaning without indicating person, tense, or number. It is the basic form of the verb: **hablar** (*to speak*), **comer** (*to eat*), **vivir** (*to live*).
In Spanish it has three different endings, **-ar**, **-er**, and **-ir**, which indicate that there are three conjugations.

22.2 Tenses and Endings

The tense of a verb indicates when something is done: past, present, or future.
The tenses are formed by changing the endings according to person and number and follow patterns that can be easily transferred from one verb to another.

■ **22.2.1** The different tenses are formed in Spanish by dropping the **-ar**, **-er**, **-ir** endings from the infinitive and adding to the stem the appropriate endings for each tense—when (in time)—and person (who is involved).

infinitive	stem	tenses	
hablar	**habl-**	**habló**	*s/he spoke*
comer	**com-**	**comían**	*they used to eat*
vivir	**viv-**	**vivo**	*I live*

In the case of the future the endings are added to the complete infinitive form including the endings **-ar**, **-er**, **-ir**:

    habl-**ar**   *to speak*
    habl-ar-**é**   *I will speak*

■ **22.2.2** In Spanish there are two kinds of tense, simple and compound.

- Simple: a part of the verb made up of one word, such as **hablaron** (*they spoke*).

- Compound: a part made up of two words, such as **he hablado** (*I have spoken*).

22.3 Person

The person of a verb indicates who is doing something:

```
Singular
1st    yo (I)
2nd    tú (you)
3rd    él (he), ella (she), usted (you formal)
```

```
Plural
1st    nosotros/nosotras (we)
2nd    vosotros/vosotras (you)
3rd    ellos (they), ellas (they), ustedes (you formal)
```

Verb endings alone are enough to tell us the subject of the verb; therefore **yo** (*I*), **tú** (*you*), etc., are usually omitted.

22.4 Mood

The moods of a verb are the forms that express a particular attitude toward what is being said. In Spanish there are two moods: indicative and subjunctive.
The indicative states facts and the subjunctive expresses wishes, doubts, possibilities, etc.

Indicative	Subjunctive
Voy al cine.	Quiero que **vayas** al cine.
I go to the movie.	*I want you to go to the movie.*

23 The Present Tense

The present tense is formed by substituting the infinitive endings -ar, -er, and -ir with the corresponding endings.

23.1 Regular Verb Pattern

	-ar	-er	-ir
yo	habl-**o**	com-**o**	viv-**o**

For full conjugation see section 41.

23.2 Radical-Changing Verbs

Most irregularities in the present tense occur in the stem while the endings are the same as for the regular verbs. For full conjugation of irregular verbs see section 42.

■ 23.2.1 Verbs that Change the Vowel

• **e → ie**   querer: quiero

Some verbs that follow the same pattern are:
-ar: **cerrar** (*to close*), **empezar** (*to start*), **pensar** (*to think*), **comenzar** (*to commence*).

-er: **entender** (*to understand*), **perder** (*to lose*).

-ir: **divertir** (*to enjoy*), **preferir** (*to prefer*), **sentir** (*to feel*).

• **o → ue**   volver: vuelvo

Some verbs that follow the same pattern are:
-ar: **contar** (*to tell*), **encontrar** (*to find*), **costar** (*to cost*).

-er: **poder** (*to be able*), **doler** (*to hurt*).

-ir: **dormir** (*to sleep*), **morir** (*to die*).

• **u → ue**   jugar: juego

- **e → i**   This only affects the -ir verbs: pedir: pido—pides

  Some verbs that present this irregularity are: **repetir** (*to repeat*), **seguir** (*to follow*), **servir** (*to serve*), **vestir** (*to dress*).

■ **23.2.2** Verbs that Change the Consonant
Some irregular verbs change their consonant. This happens only in the first person singular in the following verbs:

- **c → zc**   conducir: condu**zc**o—conduces

  Some other verbs of this kind: **parecer** (*to appear*), **ofrecer** (*to offer*), **traducir** (*to translate*).

- **c → g**   hacer: ha**g**o—haces
- Some verbs add a consonant to the stem:
  l → lg   salir: sal**g**o—sales

  n → ng   poner: pon**g**o—pones

■ **23.2.3** Irregular Changes to Spelling
Verbs that change by adding the consonant **g** in the first person only, while there is a vowel change in all other persons:

tener: ten**g**o—tienes	decir: di**g**o—dices
venir: ven**g**o—vienes	oír: oi**g**o—oyes

Similar to **oír** but with the change **e** to **ig** in the first person are:

traer: tra**ig**o—traes	caer: ca**ig**o—caes

Note that there is no root change in other persons in these verbs.

Other verbs that change their vowel or consonant in the first person singular but that are regular otherwise:

saber: **sé**—sabes	caber: **quepo**—cabes

A few verbs are completely irregular in all persons. For these verbs see section 42.

   ir: **voy—vas**   ser: **soy—eres**   haber: **he—has**

Some verbs add -y in the first person singular:

   ir: voy   ser: soy   estar: estoy   dar: doy

23.3 Use of the Present Tense

The present tense expresses the action that is happening at the moment:

   Voy a la oficina.   *I'm going to the office.*

■ **23.3.1** It expresses habitual actions:

   Voy a la playa todos los   *I go to the beach every summer.*
   veranos.

■ **23.3.2** It can also be used to express the past. This is mainly used in literary and journalistic language and to express historical events:

   En 1881 nace Picasso   *In 1881 Picasso is born in*
   en Málaga.   *Malaga.*

■ **23.3.3** The present tense can also have a future meaning indicated by the use of a time adverb:

   Mañana voy de vacaciones.   *Tomorrow I'm going on vacation.*

■ **23.3.4** It expresses actions that have no time limit:

   Esta planta crece mucho.   *This plant grows a lot.*

■ **23.3.5** It can replace the imperative to express an order:

   Tú te callas.   *You, be quiet.*

23.4 The Present Progressive

The present progressive can only refer to an action that is actually taking place or is in progress at the time of speaking:

Estoy comiendo.   *I'm eating.*
Estoy estudiando en la   *I'm studying at the university.*
universidad.

■ **23.4.1** It is formed with the present of the verb **estar** (*to be*) and the gerund (*-ing*) of the verb:

	present		-ar	-er	-ir
yo	estoy	+	cen-**ando**/com-**iendo**/viv-**iendo**		
I	am		*dining / eating / living*		

■ **23.4.2** Often the progressive and the nonprogressive forms are interchangeable:

¿Qué hace? Estudia/Está   *What is he doing? He's studying*
estudiando en su cuarto.   *in his room.*

■ **23.4.3** The progressive form is used more often when the action is perceived to be ongoing or in progress or to be repetitive.

Está leyendo.   *He's reading.*
Luis está jugando al tenis.   *Luis is playing tennis.*

■ **23.4.4** The progressive form of the present is not used with certain verbs: **estar** (*to be*), **ir** (*to go*), **venir** (*to come*), **volver** (*to return*), **regresar** (*to return*), **andar** (*to walk*), **ser** (*to be*).

24 The Future Tense

The future tense is formed by adding the future endings to the complete form of the infinitive. The endings are the same for the three conjugations.

24.1 Regular Verb Pattern

yo   habl-**é**   comer-**é**   vivir-**é**

For full conjugation see section 41.

24.2 Irregular Verbs in the Future

There are only a few irregular verbs in the future and they can be grouped as follows:

■ **24.2.1** Verbs that change the root by adding a -**d**:

tener: ten**d**ré   poner: pon**d**ré
venir: ven**d**ré   salir: sal**d**ré

■ **24.2.2** Verbs that drop the -**e** from the root when forming the future:

saber: sabré   haber: habré
poder: podré   caber: cabré

■ **24.2.3** Those that have completely irregular forms:

decir: diré   querer: querré
hacer: haré

24.3 Use of the Future

■ **24.3.1** The future expresses an action that will happen later than the time in which we are speaking:

Mi hermano **llegará** mañana.   *My brother will arrive tomorrow.*

■ **24.3.2** It can also give an action the sense/meaning of probability:

¿Qué hora es? No sé, serán las dos de la tarde.

What time is it? I don't know, it's probably about two in the afternoon.

■ **24.3.3** It can have an imperative meaning that implies a promise:

No te preocupes, **irás** a la fiesta.

Don't worry, you will go to the party.

For uses of the present with future meaning see 23.3.3

24.4 *Ir + a +* Infinitive

This is another way of conveying the future:

Voy a salir.   *I'm going out.*

It is interchangeable with the future tense:

Voy a ir de vacaciones la semana próxima.
Iré de vacaciones la semana próxima.

I'm going on vacation next week.

25 The Preterite

The preterite, or simple past, is a past tense formed by taking the endings from the infinitive and adding the preterite endings.

25.1 Regular Verb Pattern

| yo | habl-é | com-í | viv-í |

For full conjugation see section 41.

25.2 Irregular Preterite Forms: Strong Preterites

Strong preterites are irregular in all persons. The root changes and the endings form a regular pattern but are different from the regular endings.

The main difference is based on the stress. In the irregular preterites the stress is on the root, while in the regular preterites the stress is on the ending.

Strong preterites can be divided into five main groups. For full conjugation see section 42.

■ **25.2.1** Verbs that change the root vowel to **u**:
poder: pude saber: supe poner: puse haber: hube

■ **25.2.2** Verbs that change the root vowel to **i**:
decir: dije hacer: hice querer: quise venir: vine

■ **25.2.3** Verbs that add **uv** at the end of the root:
estar: estuve andar: anduve

■ **25.2.4** Verbs that add the consonant **j**:
traer: traje decir: dije conducir: conduje

■ **25.2.5** There are three verbs that are completely different in the preterite.

Dar (*to give*), which is conjugated like an **-er** or **-ir** verb:

> dar: **di**

and **ser** and **ir**, which both have the same form in the preterite: ser/ir: **fui**

25.3 Use of the Preterite

■ **25.3.1** This tense expresses finished or completed actions that happened in the past in relation to the moment of speaking:

> **Estuve** un mes en Lima.   *I was in Lima for a month.*

■ **25.3.2** Sometimes the preterite indicates the start of an action that began in the past:

> **Empezó** a trabajar el   *He began to work last year.*
> año pasado.

■ **25.3.3** It is usually accompanied by adverbs or expressions of time such as **ayer** (*yesterday*), **el año pasado** (*last year*), etc.

■ **25.3.4** In Latin America there is a preference for its use. The present perfect is not used so often. See 28.2.

26   The Imperfect

The imperfect is formed by dropping the infinitive endings, **-ar**, **-er**, **-ir**, and adding the imperfect endings to the root of the verb.

26.1 Regular Verb Pattern

yo   habl-**aba**   com-**ía**   viv-**ía**

For full conjugation see section 41.

26.2 Irregular Verbs in the Imperfect

See section 42 for the full conjugation of irregular verbs. There are only two irregular verbs: **ser** (*to be*) and **ir** (*to go*).

ser: **era**   ir: **iba**

Note that **ver** (*to see*) is slightly irregular as it keeps the **e** from the infinitive ending: ver: veía

26.3 Use of the Imperfect

■ **26.3.1** The imperfect expresses an action in the past but it does not give information about the beginning or the end of the action, either because it has not finished or the speaker is not interested in that aspect of the action:

Cantaba en la radio.   *He was singing on the radio.*

■ **26.3.2** It also expresses duration. For the speaker the duration of an action is the most important aspect. The imperfect is often used in this case accompanied by the time adverb **antes**:

Antes vivía en San Juan.   *Before, I lived (used to live) in San Juan.*

■ **26.3.3** The imperfect describes a habitual action in the past, or an action that was repeated an unspecified number of times. The English equivalent is the form *used to*:

Todos los días **se bañaba**	*Every day he used to bathe*
a las once.	*at eleven.*
Comía en este restaurante	*She often used to eat in this*
a menudo.	*restaurant.*

However, if the number of times that an action was repeated is specified then the preterite is used:

| **Fuimos cuatro o cinco** | *We went four or five times to the* |
| **veces** al teatro. | *theater.* |

■ **26.3.4** The imperfect is used to describe places, objects, and people in the past:

| El hombre **era** alto, **tenía** | *The man was tall, had blue* |
| ojos azules y **llevaba** gafas. | *eyes, and wore glasses.* |

■ **26.3.5** Background descriptions (secondary actions and circumstances that surround the main action) are expressed in the imperfect:

Ana **preparaba** la cena,	*Ana was preparing the supper,*
fuera **llovía** mucho y,	*it was raining outside, and*
de repente **se apagó**	*suddenly the light went out.*
la luz.	

■ **26.3.6** The imperfect is a relative tense because it may express one action in relation to another.

a These actions can be simultaneous:

| **Leía** el periódico mientras | *He was reading the newspaper* |
| **comía**. | *while he ate.* |

b It is used to say that something was going on when something else happened:

Paseaba por el parque	*He was walking through the*
cuando **ocurrió** el	*park when the accident*
accidente.	*occurred.*

■ **26.3.7** The imperfect is used in formal questions and requests:

¿Qué **quería** usted?	*What did you want?*
Por favor, **quería** probarme esta falda.	*Excuse me, I wanted to try this dress on.*

■ **26.3.8** Sometimes in journalistic style the imperfect is used instead of the preterite to create a major impact:

A las dos de la tarde **atracaban** el banco y media hora después la policía **detenía** a los atracadores.	*At two in the afternoon they raided the bank and half an hour later the police arrested the raiders.*

26.4 Imperfect Progressive

The imperfect progressive is formed with the imperfect of **estar** and the gerund (*-ing* form) to emphasize that something was in progress when something else happened:

Estaba estudiando cuando María llamó por teléfono.	*I was studying when María phoned.*

27 The Conditional Tense

The conditional is formed in the same way as the future, by adding the conditional endings to the infinitive form of the verb. The endings are the same for the three conjugations and coincide with the imperfect endings of -**er** and -**ir** verbs.

27.1 Regular Verb Pattern

yo   hablar-**ía**   comer-**ía**   vivir-**ía**

For full conjugation see section 41.

27.2 Irregular Verbs in the Conditional

These are the same as the irregular verbs in the future, in that the same irregularity occurs in the root. For full conjugation see section 42.

tener: tendría	saber: sabría	decir: diría
venir: vendría	poder: podría	hacer: haría
poner: pondría	haber: habría	querer: querría
salir: saldría	caber: cabría	

27.3 Use of the Conditional

The conditional is used to express the English "would/could do something":

Me dijo que **vendría** hoy.   *He told me he would come today.*

■ **27.3.1** The conditional is also used to give advice:
Deberías dejar de fumar.   *You should give up smoking.*

■ **27.3.2** It can be used to express uncertainty and probability:
Serían las doce cuando   *It was probably twelve o'clock*
se acostó.   *when he went to bed.*

■ **27.3.3** It is used in conditional sentences:

Si hiciera buen tiempo **iríamos** a la piscina.	*If the weather was/were good we would go to the pool.*

■ **27.3.4** In polite questions and requests:

¿**Podría** usted decirme dónde está la estación?	*Could you tell me where the station is?*

28 Compound Tenses

28.1 The Present Perfect

It is formed with the present of the verb **haber** plus the participle of the conjugated verb. The participle does not vary in gender or number in Spanish:

yo   **he**   habl**ado**   com**ido**   sal**ido**

See section 42.4 for the conjugation of **haber** and section 30 on participles.

■ **28.1.1** The auxiliary verb and the past participle are always used and are inseparable; it is not possible to put any words between them.

■ **28.1.2** Sometimes **haber** can be suppressed to avoid repetition when there are two or more participles:

He comido y **cenado** en este restaurante muchas veces.	*I have lunched and dined in this restaurant many times.*

28.2 Use of the Present Perfect

■ **28.2.1** The present perfect is used to express actions that have happened in a period of time that has not finished yet. The action is finished but the time in which the action was realized isn't (this year, this month, this week, today, this morning):

Este año **he trabajado** mucho.	*This year I have worked a lot.*
Este mes **he tenido** cinco días de vacaciones.	*This month I have had five days' vacation.*

■ **28.2.2** It is used to describe recent events:

El tren **ha llegado** hace unos minutos.	*The train arrived a few minutes ago.*

■ **28.2.3** It is used in events that are important for the present or that have an effect on the present:

He perdido las llaves del coche.   *I've lost my car keys.*

■ **28.2.4** Often the preterite and the present perfect are interchangeable and their use depends on the intention of the speaker. If the speaker wants to emphasize the distance from the past action, the preterite is used, but if he or she wants to bring the action nearer to the present, the present perfect is used:

Su hermano **ha muerto**.   *His brother has died.*
Su hermano **murió**.   *His brother died.*

■ **28.2.5** If there is a time barrier (the night, the weekend, etc.) the preterite is used:

La semana pasada **tuve** tres días de vacaciones.   *Last week I had three days' vacation.*
El año pasado **trabajé** mucho.   *Last year I worked hard.*

In Latin America the present perfect is used less than the preterite. The preterite is used in cases where Castilian Spanish would use the present perfect:

¿**Has traído** el regalo?   *Have you brought the present?*
¿**Trajiste** el regalo?   *Did you bring the present?*

28.3 The Past Perfect

■ **28.3.1** The past perfect, or pluperfect, is formed with the imperfect of the auxiliary verb **haber** and the participle of the conjugated verb:

yo   **había**   habl**ado**   com**ido**   sal**ido**

■ **28.3.2** The past perfect is the past of the past. It corresponds to the English *had done something*. It is used in speech about past actions to describe other actions that preceded them and are relevant to them:

| Cuando **llegué**, el | *When I arrived the restaurant* |
| restaurante **había cerrado**. | *had closed.* |

28.4 The Preterite Perfect

■ **28.4.1** The preterite perfect is formed with the preterite, or simple past, of the auxiliary verb **haber** and the past participle of the conjugated verb:

| yo | **hube** | habl**ado** | com**ido** | sal**ido** |

■ **28.4.2** It is mainly used in literary texts and hardly used in spoken Spanish. It corresponds to the English *had done something*. It expresses an action completed just before another past action:

| Cuando **hubo callado**, | *When he had stopped talking,* |
| hablé yo. | *I spoke.* |

It is usually preceded by the time adverb **apenas**:

| **Apenas hubo llegado**, | *He had hardly arrived, when* |
| empezó la fiesta. | *the party began.* |

28.5 The Future Perfect

■ **28.5.1** This is formed with the future of the auxiliary verb **haber** and the participle of the conjugated verb:

| yo | **habré** | habl**ado** | com**ido** | sal**ido** |

■ **28.5.2** It expresses a future action in relation to another future action that will happen afterward. It is translated as *will have done something*:

Cuando lleguen al cine	*By the time they arrive at the*
ya **habré sacado** las	*movie I will have already*
entradas.	*bought the tickets.*

■ **28.5.3** It is also used to express probability in the past:

| Luis **habrá llegado** tarde. | *Luis will have arrived late.* |

28.6 The Conditional Perfect

■ **28.6.1** It is formed with the conditional of the auxiliary verb **haber** and the participle of the conjugated verb:

| yo | **habría** | hab**lado** | com**ido** | sal**ido** |

■ **28.6.2** It corresponds to the English *would have done something*. It is used to say what would have happened:

Dijo que cuando terminara sus estudios ya **habría encontrado** trabajo.
He said that when he had finished his studies he would have already found work.

■ **28.6.3** It also forms part of conditional perfect sentences linked to *if* plus the past perfect subjunctive:

Si hubieras llamado **habría salido** contigo.
If you had called I would have gone out with you.

28.7 Compound Tenses of the Subjunctive

■ **28.7.1** The Present Perfect Subjunctive
It is formed with the present subjunctive of the verb **haber** plus the participle of the conjugated verb. The participle does not vary in gender or number.

| yo | **haya** | hab**lado** | com**ido** | sal**ido** |

■ **28.7.2** The Past Perfect Subjunctive
The past perfect (or pluperfect) subjunctive is formed with the imperfect subjunctive of the auxiliary verb **haber** and the participle of the conjugated verb:

| yo | **hubiera/hubiese** | hab**lado** | com**ido** | sal**ido** |

It corresponds to the English *had done something* after *if*:

Si **hubiera estudiado** más habría aprobado el examen.
If he had studied more he would have passed the exam.

For the subjunctive see section 33.

29 The Infinitive

The Spanish infinitive is the most basic form of the verb and the starting point for all other forms. Grammatically it expresses meaning without indicating person, tense, or number. Infinitives are words like **cenar** (*to dine*), **comer** (*to eat*), **escribir** (*to write*).

29.1 Form

The infinitive identifies the three verb categories (conjugations) of the Spanish verb by its three different endings:

-ar	-er	-ir
habl-**ar**	com-**er**	escrib-**ir**

■ **29.1.1** The compound infinitive is: **haber** + participle of the conjugated verb:

haber estudiado	*to have studied*
haber comido	*to have eaten*
haber salido	*to have left/gone out*

29.2 Use of the Infinitive

■ **29.2.1** The infinitive can act as a verb but also as a noun. As a noun it is considered masculine and singular:

Hacer ejercicio es bueno para todos.   *Doing exercise is good for everyone.*

■ **29.2.2** The infinitive can also take an article and a demonstrative, possessive, and indefinite adjective, in the masculine form:

El viajar es un placer.   *Travel is a pleasure.*

■ **29.2.3** Some infinitives have acquired their own meanings as nouns and can appear in the plural:

el deber, los deberes   *duty, duties*

For use of the infinitive with modal verbs see section 39, and with phrasal verbs see section 38.1. For constructions like **gustar** + the infinitive see section 36. See section 9.1 for use of personal pronouns with the infinitive.

29.3 Prepositions + Infinitive

After certain prepositions the infinitive is used to make some useful expressions:

■ **29.3.1** Adjectives + **de** + infinitive:
Es **fácil** de hacer.   *It's easy to do.*

■ **29.3.2** De + infinitive has a conditional value:
De haber sabido que   *If I had known you were*
venías habría terminado   *coming I would have finished*
antes.   *earlier.*

■ **29.3.3** Al + infinitive refers to a specific point in time:
Al terminar la fiesta se   ***As soon as** the party*
marchó. (= Cuando terminó   *finished he left.*
la fiesta se marchó.)

It can also have a causal meaning:
Al no ver a sus amigos   ***As she could not see** her*
se marchó. (= Como no vio a   *friends, she left.*
sus amigos se marchó.)

■ **29.3.4** Por + infinitive indicates an unfinished action:
Esto está **por terminar** aún.   *This is still **to be finished**.*

■ **29.3.5** A/para + infinitive expresses the purpose of an action:
Fue **a visitar** a sus padres.   *She went **to visit** her parents.*
Vino **para devolverte** el   *She came **to return** your*
libro.   *book.*

29.4 The Infinitive Used as Imperative

■ **29.4.1** The infinitive has an imperative meaning in notices, instructions, and advertisements:

Girar a la derecha.   *Turn right.*
Mezclar con agua.   *Mix with water.*

■ **29.4.2** The infinitive is used in colloquial language instead of the second person plural of the imperative:

¡**Cerrar** la puerta!   *Close the door!*

■ **29.4.3** The infinitive preceded by **a**:

¡A comer!   *Let's eat!*
¡A dormir!   *Off to bed!*

See section 38.1 for phrasal verbs with the infinitive.

30 Participles

The past participle follows **haber** in compound tenses and is also used in passive constructions.

30.1 The Past Participle Form

The past participle of regular verbs is formed by modifying the infinitive endings of each verb type as follows:

-**ar** verbs ➔ -**ado**: **hablado**
-**er** verbs ➔ -**ido**: **comido**
-**ir** verbs ➔ -**ido**: **salido**

He **cenado** con mis amigos. He **bebido** vino. He **salido** de casa a las ocho.
I had dinner with my friends. I drank wine. I left home at eight.

30.2 Irregular Past Participles

■ **30.2.1** There are many verbs with irregular participles:

Infinitive	Participle	Infinitive	Participle
abrir	**abierto**	hacer	**hecho**
escribir	**escrito**	volver	**vuelto**

He **escrito** una carta. *I have written a letter.*
Hemos **vuelto** a casa a las diez. *We got back home at ten.*

For other irregular past participles see section 42.

■ **30.2.2** Some verbs have a regular form when they act as verbs and an irregular form when they act as adjectives:

Infinitive	Adjective	Verb
confundir	confuso	confundido
despertar	despierto	despertado
soltar	suelto	soltado

Me he **despertado** a las cuatro.	*I woke up at four.*
El niño está **despierto**.	*The child is awake.*

30.3 Use of Past Participles

■ **30.3.1** The past participle is used mainly with the auxiliary verb **haber** to form compound tenses. In this case the participle is invariable:

Ha **llegado**, ha **bebido** algo y	*He arrived, drank something,*
ha **salido** inmediatamente.	*and left immediately.*

■ **30.3.2** The past participle can be used as an adjective and in this case agrees in number and gender in the same way as all adjectives:

Quiero pollo **asado**.	*I'd like roast chicken.*
Juana está **cansada**.	*Juana is tired.*

■ **30.3.3** The verb *to be* + past participle forms the passive and in this case the past participle is variable, changing in number and person:

Los chalets han sido	*The chalets have been built*
construidos cerca de la playa.	*near the beach.*

For the passive see section 34.

30.4 Absolute Participle

The absolute participle is used mainly in literary style. It often begins the sentence.

Acabada la fiesta volvieron	*When the party finished*
a casa.	*they returned home.*

30.5 Present Participle

■ **30.5.1** The present participle acts as an adjective. It is sometimes used to replace a relative clause, especially in

formal or journalistic language. The English equivalent is
the participle -*ing* form:

La situación en el país es **inquietante**.	*The situation in the country is worrying.*

■ **30.5.2** Forms:

```
-ar verbs → -ante: inquietar → inquietante  worrying
-er verbs → -ente or -iente:
           proceder → procedente  coming from
-ir verbs → -ente or -iente: sonreír → sonriente
           smiling
```

tren **procedente** de México con destino a Guadalajara	*the train from Mexico City to Guadalajara*

Note that the gerund, -**ando** or -**iendo**, which in English
corresponds to the -*ing* form, should not be used as an
adjective. See section 31 for the gerund.

The Gerund

The gerund is a verbal noun that adds meaning to the main verb. It corresponds to the form -*ing* in English. It is a form that does not admit any variations and has an adverbial function, which is that of modifying the main verb in a sentence:

> Llegó **llorando**.　　　　　*He arrived **crying**.*

Do not confuse with the present participle. See 30.5.

31.1 Forms of the Gerund

> verbs in -**ar** → -**ando**: **cantando**
> verbs in -**er** → -**iendo**: **bebiendo**
> verbs in -**ir** → -**iendo**: **escribiendo**

■ **31.1.1** The compound gerund is **habiendo** + the participle of the conjugated verb:

> habiendo cenado　　　　　*having had supper*

31.2 Use of the Gerund

■ **31.2.1** It is mainly used in the construction **estar** + gerund. This expresses the present progressive (-*ing* form) (see 23.4 on the present progressive):

> **Estoy leyendo** un libro muy interesante.　　*I'm reading a very interesting book.*

■ **31.2.2** The gerund is also used to express duration:

> Estudia **escuchando** música.　　*He studies while **listening** to music.*

■ **31.2.3** It indicates simultaneous actions:

> Y **enfadándose**, salió del cuarto.　　*And **getting angry**, he left the room.*

■ **31.2.4** The compound gerund expresses an action completed before the action expressed by the main verb:

| **Habiendo terminado** | *The class **having finished**,* |
| la clase, salimos todos. | *we all left.* |

■ **31.2.5** When the gerund acts as an adverb it expresses the manner or the way the action is carried out:

| Habla **gritando**. | *He shouts when he speaks.* |

See section 9.7 for use of the gerund with pronouns. See 38.2 on phrasal verbs for a study of special constructions with the gerund.

32 The Imperative

The imperative has four forms in Spanish—two for the familiar form (singular **tú** and plural **vosotros**) and two for the formal form (**usted** and the plural **ustedes**).

32.1 Form

The familiar forms of the imperative are as follows:

	-ar	-er	-ir
(tú)	habl-**a**	com-**e**	escrib-**e**
(vosotros)	habl-**ad**	com-**ed**	escrib-**id**

The form used for **tú** affirmative is the same as the third person singular of the present tense of the indicative.
The forms used for **usted** and **ustedes** and the negative coincide with the forms of the subjunctive:

Hab**le** más despacio.	*Speak more slowly.*
No beb**as** más.	*Don't drink anything else.*

For the subjunctive see section 33.

32.2 Imperatives Followed by Personal Pronouns

■ **32.2.1** When the pronoun is attached to the verb the stress of the word changes place and often needs an accent:

Toma la medicina.	*Take the medicine.*
Tóma**la**.	*Take **it**.*

■ **32.2.2** The imperative plural **vosotros** loses the final **-d** of its ending when it is followed by **-os**:

Despertaos a las ocho.	*Wake up at eight.*
Poneos de pie.	*Stand up.*

■ **32.2.3** The imperative form for **nosotros** loses its final ending -s when it is followed by the pronoun **nos**:

Pongámonos en la fila.   *Let's stand in the line.*
(pongamos + **nos**)

32.3 Irregular Imperatives

In the **tú** form there are the following irregular imperative forms:

salir	**sal**	*leave/go out*	**decir**	**di**	*tell*
tener	**ten**	*have/take*	**hacer**	**haz**	*make/do*
poner	**pon**	*put*	**ir**	**ve**	*go*
venir	**ven**	*come*			

32.4 Use of the Imperative

■ **32.4.1** The familiar imperative is widely used in Spain, and its use is growing. It is familiar but it is socially acceptable, and polite, especially if accompanied by "**por favor**":

Dame un café con leche,   *Give me a coffee with cream,*
por favor.   *please.*

■ **32.4.2** These forms of **tú** and **vosotros** are not used generally in Latin America, where the use of **usted** and **ustedes** is preferred:

(usted) **Pase**.   *Come in.*
(ustedes) **Salgan**   *You go out, boys.*
muchachos.

■ **32.4.3** The formal **usted** is used but is often substituted by **puedo** + infinitive:

¿**Puede cerrar** la puerta,   *Could you close the door*
por favor?   *please?*
Cierre la puerta, por favor. *Could you close the door please.*

33 The Subjunctive

The subjunctive form is widely used in Spanish. It serves to express uncertainty, possibility, and even unreality. Where the indicative expresses actions that are real or that we think are real, the subjunctive serves to express personal attitudes, wishes, doubt, hopes, orders, fear, etc.:

Juan **vendrá** mañana.	*Juan will come tomorrow.*
Quiero que Juan **venga** mañana.	*I want Juan to come tomorrow.*

The present subjunctive can express both the present and the future action and can be used in independent clauses and in subordinate clauses. Most of these subordinate clauses that have a subjunctive are introduced by **que**:

Espero **que** el tren llegue puntual.	*I hope the train comes on time.*
¡Ojalá apruebe el examen!	*I hope I pass the exam!*
Es posible que apruebe el examen.	*It's possible I'll pass the exam.*

What we say in the main clause affects whether the subordinate clause has a subjunctive or not:

Sé que **vendrá.**	*I know he'll come.*
(expresses certainty)	
Espero que **venga.**	*I hope he comes.*
(expresses hope or doubt)	

A very important rule to remember about the use of the subjunctive in Spanish is that the subject of the main clause must be different from the subject of the subordinate clause, otherwise we use the infinitive:

Quiero ir al cine.	*I want to go to the movie.*
Quiero que vayas al cine.	*I want you to go to the movie.*

33.1 Use of the Subjunctive

The subjunctive is used with the following verbs and expressions.

■ **33.1.1** Giving advice:

Les recomiendo que coman paella. — *I suggest you have the paella.*

Es mejor que te acuestes pronto. — *It's better if you go to bed early.*

■ **33.1.2** After verbs of ordering, allowing, forbidding:

Te prohíbo que salgas esta noche. — *I forbid you to go out tonight.*

¿Me permite que abra la ventana? — *Do you mind if I open the window?*

■ **33.1.3** Emotions such as wishes, likes and dislikes, hope and fear:

Quiero que me digas la verdad. — *I want you to tell me the truth.*

Me molesta que hagas tanto ruido. — *It annoys me that you make so much noise.*

Espero que te pongas bien. — *I hope you'll get better.*

¡Ojalá haga sol! — *I hope it's sunny!*

Note that **que** is not used after **ojalá**. The latter is generally used with exclamation marks.

■ **33.1.4** Necessity, using expressions such as **es necesario/ importante/conveniente que** . . . :

Es necesario que estés en la cama unos días. — *It will be necessary for you to stay in bed for a few days.*

These are equivalent to the English modal verbs *should, ought to, need to, must*.

■ **33.1.5** Possibility, probability, and doubt, using expressions such as **quizás**, **tal vez** (*perhaps*), and **es**

probable/posible/puede ser que . . . :

Es probable que vea a Luis.	*Probably I'll see Luis.*
Quizás vaya a Panamá el año que viene.	*Perhaps I'll go to Panama next year.*

Note that **quizá(s)** and **tal vez** are not followed by **que**.

■ **33.1.6** After the negative form of knowing, perceiving, stating, and communicating:

- If the main clause expressing an opinion, a statement, knowledge, or perception is positive (**creer que**, **opinar que**, **decir que**, **es verdad que**, **es cierto que**, etc.), the verb in the subordinate clause is in the indicative.

- However, if the main clause is in the negative, it is necessary to use a subjunctive in the subordinate clause as it conveys the meaning of doubt or uncertainty:

Indicative	Subjunctive
Creo que es artista.	**No creo que sea** artista.
I think he's an artist.	*I don't think he's an artist.*
Me parece que trabaja mucho.	**No me parece que trabaje** mucho.
I think she works hard.	*I don't think she works very hard.*

33.2 The Subjunctive After Subordinators

The subjunctive is needed after the following expressions.

■ **33.2.1** Intention and purpose, after **para que**, **a fin de que**, **con el propósito de que**, **con la intención de que**, etc.:

Traigo este libro **para que lo lea** tu hijo.	*I'm bringing this book so that your son can read it.*

■ **33.2.2** Temporary expressions, after **cuando**, **hasta que**, **antes de que**, **mientras (que)**, **tan pronto como**, **en cuanto**, etc.:

Cuando salga el sol iremos a la playa. — *When the sun comes out we'll go to the beach.*

Me arreglaré **antes de que venga**. — *I'll get ready before she comes.*

■ **33.2.3** Result, aim, and manner, after **de manera que**, **de modo que** (indicating a purpose), **sin que** (*without*):

Habla más fuerte **de modo que todos te oigamos**. — *Speak louder so we all can hear you.*

Saldré **sin que me vea**. — *I'll leave without him seeing me.*

■ **33.2.4** **Como** requires a subjunctive in the expression **como + querer** meaning *as you like*, when it refers to an action that still has not happened:

Vístete **como quieras**. — *Dress as you like.*

■ **33.2.5** Condition, after **con tal (de que)**, **siempre y cuando** (*provided that*), **a condición de que** (*on condition that*):

Te llevaré conmigo **a condición de que te portes** bien. — *I'll take you with me on condition that you behave well.*

■ **33.2.6** Exception, after **excepto que**, **salvo que**, **a no ser que** (*unless*):

Iremos al campo este fin de semana **a no ser que esté** muy ocupado. — *We'll go to the countryside this weekend unless I'm very busy.*

■ **33.2.7** Concession, after **aunque**, **aun cuando** (*although*), **a pesar de que** (*despite the fact that*), **por más que**, **por mucho que.**

Note that the subjunctive is used when the event is in the future. Otherwise the indicative is used:

Aunque tenga mucho trabajo irá de vacaciones. *Even if he has a lot of work he'll go on vacation.*
(He might or might not have a lot of work.)

Compare with:

Aunque tiene mucho trabajo irá de vacaciones. *Although he has a lot of work, he will go on vacation.*
(He has a lot of work, but despite that he will go on vacation.)

33.3 The Subjunctive in Relative Clauses

■ **33.3.1** Relative pronoun + the subjunctive is used when the event of the main clause is not yet known in expressions such as:

El que llegue antes, que prepare la cena. *Whoever arrives first prepares supper.*
No hay **quien te entienda**. *There's nobody who can understand you.*

■ **33.3.2** **Lo que**, meaning *whatever*, **lo que quieras** (*whatever you want*), **lo que tú digas** (*whatever you say*):

Haré **lo que tú digas**. *I'll do whatever you say.*
Haz **lo que quieras**. *Do what you like.*

33.4 The Subjunctive in Main Clauses

Although the subjunctive is used mainly in subordinate clauses, it is used in main clauses, usually with an imperative meaning:

¡Entre! *Come in!*

It is also used in idiomatic expressions:

¡Dígame! *Hello! (on the phone)*

Que followed by a subjunctive indicates an order:

¡Que venga!	*He must come!*
¡Que salga!	*Make him leave!*
¡Que pase!	*Tell him to come in.*

Note that there are no accents on the **que**. For the subjunctive as an imperative see section 32.1 on imperatives.

There are many complexities concerning the subjunctive. The examples given here are by no means exclusive. A good book on Spanish verbs should help in-depth study.

33.5 The Imperfect Subjunctive

■ **33.5.1** When the main clause is in the present or future tense the present subjunctive is used. When the main verb is in the preterite, imperfect, or conditional the imperfect subjunctive is used:

Yo te aconsejo que **tomes** unas vacaciones.	*I advise you to take a vacation.*
Yo te aconsejé que **tomaras** unas vacaciones.	*I advised you to take a vacation.*
Me gustaría que **tomaras** unas vacaciones.	*I would like you to take a vacation.*

■ **33.5.2** The imperfect subjunctive is used after **si** in conditional sentences such as *if I had/were . . . I would . . .*:

Si tuviera dinero me compraría un coche.	*If I had money I would buy myself a car.*

33.6 The Past Perfect Subjunctive

■ **33.6.1** The past perfect (or pluperfect) subjunctive is mainly used after **si** in conditional perfect sentences. The second part of the conditional clause is a conditional perfect:

Si hubiera tenido dinero   *If I had had money I would have*
habría ido de vacaciones.   *gone on vacation.*

33.7 Forms of the Subjunctive

■ 33.7.1 Present

The present subjunctive is formed by removing the **-o**
ending from the first person singular of the present
indicative and adding the endings of the subjunctive:

   yo   habl-**e**   com-**a**   viv-**a**

For full conjugation see section 41.

All the irregularities that affect the stem only in the first
person singular in the present indicative affect the present
subjunctive in all the persons:

salir	
yo **salg**-a	nosotros/as **salg**-amos
tú **salg**-as	vosotros/as **salg**-áis
él/ella/Ud. **salg**-a	ellos/ellas/Uds. **salg**-an

See section 42 on irregular verbs. Note that in
radical-changing verbs the irregularity does not
affect the first and second persons plural:

querer	
yo **quier**-a	nosotros/as **quer**-amos
tú quier-as	vosotros/as **quer**-áis
él/ella/Ud. quier-a	ellos/ellas/Uds. quier-an

See radical-changing verbs in section 23.2.

■ 33.7.2 Exceptions in Radical-Changing Verbs

- Verbs ending in **-ir** that have **e** as a radical vowel, change the **e** into **i** including the first and second persons plural:
  pedir: **pid**amos—**pid**áis

- The verbs **morir** and **dormir** change the radical **o** into **u** in the first and second persons plural:
  dormir: **durm**amos—**durm**áis

- **Jugar** keeps the radical **u** in the first and second persons plural:
  jugar: **jugu**emos—**jugu**éis

■ 33.7.3 Irregular Verbs

The verbs **dar**, **haber**, **ir**, **saber**, and **caber** are completely irregular and the irregularity of the first person occurs in the rest (for full conjugation see section 42):

dar: dé—des	**ir:** vaya—vayas
haber: haya—hayas	**saber:** sepa—sepas

33.8 Other Tenses of the Subjunctive

■ 33.8.1 The Imperfect Subjunctive

The imperfect subjunctive has a peculiarity unique in the Spanish verb system in that it has two endings that are used in exactly the same way.

This tense is formed by adding its endings to the stem of the preterite (indicative). All the verbs with irregularities in this tense have the same irregularity in the imperfect subjunctive. See section 41 for conjugation of regular verbs and section 42 for conjugation of irregular verbs.

-ar: yo	habl**ara**	or	habl**ase**
-er: yo	com**iera**	or	com**iese**
-ir: yo	viv**iera**	or	viv**iese**

Note that verbs with **y** or **j** (**construir, decir**, etc.) in the third person singular of the preterite add **-era/-ese** instead of **-iera/-iese**:

construyó: construy**era**/construy**ese**

dijo: dij**era**/dij**ese**

Ser and **ir** are special in that the form is the same for both and they also use **-era/-ese**: **fuera** or **fuese**.

■ **33.8.2** Compound Forms in the Subjunctive

The present perfect subjunctive is formed with the present subjunctive of the auxiliary verb **haber** plus the participle of the conjugated verb. See section 42.4 for conjugation of **haber**.

yo	**haya**	hablado	comido	salido

The pluperfect subjunctive is formed with the imperfect subjunctive of the auxiliary verb **haber** and the participle of the conjugated verb:

yo	**hubiera/ hubiese**	hablado	comido	salido

34 The Passive

When something is done to the subject, not by the subject, the verb is said to be in the passive voice.

The passive in Spanish can be expressed in different ways. It is formed with the verb **ser** (*to be*) and the past participle of the verb. This past participle agrees in number and gender with the subject of the clause.

The agent of the action is preceded by the preposition **por**:

La carta fue escrita **por** el director.	*The letter was written by the director.*
La niña será operada **por** un médico excelente.	*The girl will be operated on by an excellent doctor.*

34.1 Impersonal Form with Passive Meaning

When the agent is unknown the passive construction is often replaced by the impersonal form *they* by using the third person plural of the verb:

La catedral **fue construida** en 1765.	*The cathedral was built in 1765.*
Construyeron la catedral en 1765.	*They built the cathedral in 1765.*

34.2 The Passive with *Ser*

The passive with **ser** is used mainly in written language, especially of a journalistic kind, and it is used more in Latin American Spanish:

Los ladrones **fueron detenidos** ayer.	*The thieves were arrested yesterday.*

34.3 Passive Constructions with *Se*

Another way of expressing the passive is the construction with **se**. The action itself is considered to be of most importance, and not the person who carries it out. The

person is not included in the sentence in these cases.
It is formed with the pronoun **se** plus the third person of
the conjugated verb (singular or plural, depending on
whether the subject is singular or plural):

Se construyó esta casa hace dos años.	*This house was built two years ago.*
Se enviaron los documentos por correo aéreo.	*The documents were sent by airmail.*

Note that the subject can be placed before or after the verb:

Esta casa **se construyó** hace dos años.	*This house was built two years ago.*

This construction is preferred when the human agent is
absent and the subject is a thing.
It can be substituted by a passive with **ser**:

Esta casa **fue construida** hace dos años.	*This house was built two years ago.*

34.4 Impersonal *Se*

The construction for this is the same as above, but with the
emphasis on the fact that the agent is indeterminate and
generic and is not mentioned in the clause:

Se vende piso.	*Condominium for sale.*

■ **34.4.1** In this impersonal construction with **se** the
passive with **ser** is not a possible substitute.

En México **se bebe** mucha cerveza.	*In Mexico a lot of beer is drunk.*
En este restaurante **se come** muy bien.	*In this restaurant you eat well.*

■ **34.4.2** It is possible to substitute the impersonal **se** by
generic and indefinite pronouns such as **alguien**, **uno**,
gente, or by the verb in the first or third person plural:

Se alquila apartamento.	*Apartment to rent.*
= **Alquilan** apartamento.	
Se come bien aquí.	*One eats well here.*
= **Uno come** bien/**comemos** bien aquí.	

■ **34.4.3** When the direct object of the impersonal clause is a person it must be preceded by the preposition **a**. In this case the verb is always singular as it is an impersonal construction:

Se busca **a** este hombre.	*Wanted: this man.*

■ **34.4.4** Verbs followed by the infinitive are in the singular:

Se pretende resolver estos problemas pronto.	*It is intended to resolve these problems soon.*

But the verbs **querer, poder, tener que, deber, haber de,** or **acabar de** change to the plural if the subject is plural:

Se quieren solucionar **los problemas** pronto.	*They want to solve these problems soon.*

■ **34.4.5** **Uno** must be used instead of **se** with verbs that are already constructed with **se**, such as reflexives:

Con este calor se cansa **uno** enseguida.	*With this heat one gets tired quickly.*

34.5 Idiomatic Sentences with *Se*

There are several idiomatic sentences that use the impersonal **se** followed by a whole subordinate clause. In these cases the verb is always singular:

se ve que	*one sees that*
se dice que	*it is said that*
se cree que	*it is believed that*
se espera que	*it is hoped that*

35 Pronominal Verbs

Pronominal verbs are verbs accompanied by an object pronoun that is the same as the subject of the sentence. There are many different kinds of pronominal verbs, and Spanish has a tendency to use pronouns with verbs even when they are not necessary:

Se comió toda la sopa.   *He ate all the soup.*

35.1 The Reflexive Verb

See section 10 on reflexive pronouns.
In a reflexive sentence the subject both does and receives the action. It does something to or for him/her/itself. Reflexive verbs are accompanied by reflexive pronouns:

Me ducho por la mañana. *I take a shower in the morning.*
                            (I shower myself.)

■ **35.1.1** With some verbs the reflexive construction in Spanish has the meaning of having something done instead of doing something for oneself:

Ana **se** corta el pelo en la   *Ana has her hair cut at Rizos,*
peluquería Rizos.   *the hairdresser's.*
Juan **se** construyó un   *Juan had a hut built on the*
cabaña en la playa.   *beach.*

Sometimes there is ambiguity in the meaning:

Isabel **se** va a hacer un   *Isabel is going to make a dress*
vestido para la boda.   *for the wedding.*

This sentence could have two meanings. *Isabel is going to make the dress herself* or *Isabel is going to have her dress made by someone else*. To avoid the confusion sometimes it is possible to add the subject pronoun and **mismo** or **solo**:

Isabel **se** va a hacer un   *Isabel is going to make a dress*
vestido **ella misma**.   *herself.*

35.2 Reciprocal Verbs

A pronominal verb can have a reciprocal meaning when an action or feeling refers back to the person/s concerned:

Los hermanos **se** quieren mucho.	*The brothers love each other a lot.*
Juan y Marta **se** enamoraron.	*Juan and Marta fell in love with each other.*

Sometimes the expression **el uno al otro/los unos a los otros** is added for clarity or emphasis:

Se miraron **el uno al otro**.	*They looked at each other.*

35.3 Other Verbs with a Pronominal Form

■ **35.3.1** Several verbs can be used with or without the reflexive:

Bañaré a la niña y después **me bañaré** yo.	*I'll bathe the baby and after I'll take a bath myself.*

■ **35.3.2** But many verbs, such as **arrepentirse**, **quejarse**, **atreverse**, only have the reflexive form:

Mi hermano **se quejó** del servicio en aquel hotel.	*My brother complained about the service in that hotel.*

■ **35.3.3** Some verbs have the two forms but their meaning is very different:

cambiar	*to change*	cambiarse	*to get changed*
aburrir	*to bore*	aburrirse	*to get bored*
molestar	*to bother*	molestarse	*to be bothered*

35.4 Pronominal Verbs with Special Meanings

■ **35.4.1** **Ponerse** means *to become, to get.* It is used with adjectives to indicate changes of a temporary nature. This construction tends to be used more than alternative verbs with the same meaning:

ponerse enfermo	enfermar	*to become sick*
ponerse triste	entristecerse	*to become sad*
ponerse gordo	engordar	*to become fat*

■ **35.4.2 Volverse** means *to become, to go*. It indicates psychological change in people. It describes a more permanent change than **ponerse**:

volverse loco	*to go mad*
volverse agresivo	*to become aggressive*

It also means a change in circumstances:

La situación **se ha vuelto** imposible.	*The situation has become impossible.*

■ **35.4.3 Hacerse** means *to become* but in a professional, political, or religious context. It implies voluntary change:

hacerse profesor	*to become a teacher*

■ **35.4.4 Convertirse en** means *to become, to turn into*:

La televisión **se ha convertido en** algo esencial en el hogar.	*The television has become something essential to the home.*

■ **35.4.5 Quedarse** means *to remain, to be left*:

quedarse viudo	*to be left as a widower*
quedarse solo	*to remain alone*

Quedarse can also have other meanings such as *to stay*:

Me quedaré en la playa.	*I'll stay on the beach.*

35.5 Other Verbs with Pronoun as Intensifier

■ **35.5.1** There are some verbs in Spanish that do not

need a reflexive pronoun but have adopted one to emphasize the power of the verb. They focus on the verb without really changing the meaning. This often happens with verbs of motion such as **irse**, **marcharse**, **volverse**, **salirse**, **subirse**, **bajarse**, **escaparse**, and **caerse**:

¡Hasta luego! **Me voy**.	*See you later. I'm going.*
Mañana **me marcharé** a Nueva York.	*Tomorrow I'm off to New York.*
La botella **se cayó** de la mesa.	*The bottle fell from the table.*

■ **35.5.2** With verbs of consumption such as **tomarse**, **comerse**, and **beberse**:

Se bebió un vaso de vino y **se comió** un poco de jamón.
He drank a glass of wine and ate a little ham.

■ **35.5.3** Also with verbs that indicate perception and knowledge:

¿**Te sabes** la lección?	*Do you know the lesson?*
Sí, **me la he aprendido** enseguida.	*Yes, I learned it in no time.*

■ **35.5.4** With **morirse**, which means *to die a natural death*:

Juan **se murió** de viejo.	*Juan died an old man.*
Juan **murió** en un accidente.	*Juan died in an accident.*

■ **35.5.5** With **creerse**, **olvidarse**, **reírse**:

Me creí todo lo que me dijo.	*I believed everything he told me.*
Me olvidé de llamar a María.	*I forgot to call María.*
Se ríe de todo.	*He laughs at everything.*

For other pronominal constructions, especially with **se**, see section 10 and section 34 on the passive.

36.1 *Gustar*

There is a special construction in Spanish that is the opposite in form to its equivalent in English. The subject in the Spanish construction is the object in the English one and the subject in English becomes the object in Spanish:

Me gusta la comida mexicana.	*I like Mexican food.* (Literally: *Mexican food pleases me.*)

■ **36.1.1** These constructions are formed with the personal pronoun followed by a verb used in the third person singular or plural depending on the word that follows, which can be a noun or an infinitive:

personal pronoun	verb	noun
Me	**gusta**	**el vino tinto.**

personal pronoun	verb	infinitive
Nos	**gusta**	**salir por la noche.**

If **me gusta** (or any other verb of this type) is followed by one or more verbs in the infinitive, it always appears in the singular:

Me gusta salir y divertirme. *I like going out and enjoying myself.*

■ **36.1.2** Sometimes the noun or the infinitive clause are placed at the beginning of the sentence:

Este abrigo me gusta. *I like this coat.*

36.2 Other Verbs like *Gustar*

The verbs that follow this rule are **encantar**, **interesar**, **importar**, **doler**, **faltar**, and **quedar**:

Me encantan las películas románticas.	*I love romantic films.*

37 Impersonal Verbs

Impersonal verbs are those that are only conjugated in the third person singular.

37.1 Impersonal Verbs in Weather Expressions

llover	Llueve.	*It's raining.*
nevar	Nieva.	*It's snowing.*
amanecer	Amanece.	*It's getting light.*

37.2 *Hay, Hace, Es*

The verbs **haber**, **hacer**, and **ser** also have impersonal forms in the third person.

■ **37.2.1** **Hay** (*there is, there are*) from **haber**:

En el pueblo **hay** un mercado y **hay** muchas tiendas.	*In the village there is a market and there are a lot of shops.*

■ **37.2.2** **Hacer** in weather expressions:

Hace frío.	*It's cold.*
Hace calor.	*It's hot.*

■ **37.2.3** **Hacer** in expressions of time:

Hace + time + **que** + verb

Hace dos años **que** vivo aquí.	*I've lived here for two years.*
Hace cinco meses **que** empezó a estudiar español.	*He began to study Spanish five months ago.*

■ **37.2.4** **Hacer falta**:

No **hace falta** hacer reserva.	*It's not necessary to make a reservation.*

■ **37.2.5 Ser** used in expressions of time:
Es pronto.	*It's soon.*
Es temprano.	*It's early.*
Es tarde.	*It's late.*

37.3 Other Impersonal Constructions with *Ser*

Es mejor (que):
Es mejor callarse.	*It's better to keep quiet.*
Es mejor que tomen el autobús.	*It's better if they take the bus.*

Es importante:
Es importante llegar puntual.	*It's important to arrive punctually.*

For more of these see section 33 on the subjunctive and section 34 on the passive.

37.4 Impersonal Constructions with Other Verbs

Faltar:
Faltan dos minutos para empezar la carrera.	*The race starts in two minutes.*
Falta pintar el comedor.	*We need to paint the dining room.*

Parecer que:
Parece que va a llover.	*It looks as though it is going to rain.*

Valer más:
Más vale que llames antes de ir a su casa.	*It's better if you phone before you go to his house.*

For impersonal constructions and sentences with impersonal **se** see section 34.

38 Phrasal Verbs

Phrasal verbs are formed with an auxiliary verb followed by either the infinitive, the gerund, or the participle. The form gives the meaning and the auxiliary verb gives the information about the person, tense, and number.

38.1 Phrasal Verbs with the Infinitive

■ **38.1.1 Acabar de** + the infinitive expresses an action that has just happened or one in the immediate past:

El tren **acaba de salir**.	*The train has just left.*
Acababa de salir cuando llegaron.	*It had just left when they arrived.*

■ **38.1.2 Ir a** + the infinitive expresses an action about to take place or one in the immediate future. It sometimes expresses intention. It is often interchangeable with the future form:

Voy a salir esta tarde con mis amigos.	*I'm going to go out this afternoon with my friends.*
Voy a ir de vacaciones dentro de unos días.	*I'm going on vacation in a few days.*

■ **38.1.3 Volver a** + the infinitive expresses repetition or the idea of doing something again:

Volvió a empezar. (= empezó de nuevo)	*He started again.*

■ **38.1.4 Ponerse a** + the infinitive indicates the beginning of an action.

Todos los días **se pone a estudiar** a las seis.	*Every day he starts studying at six.*

■ **38.1.5** **Echar/echarse a** + the infinitive express the beginning of a sudden action, taken in a decisive manner:

El niño **echó a andar**, *The boy started walking but he*
pero se cayó y **se echó** *fell and started crying.*
a llorar.

■ **38.1.6** **Quedar en** + the infinitive expresses obligation when the subject is singular:

Quedó en llamarnos *She arranged to call us at ten.*
a las diez.

Also, when the subject is plural, it expresses the agreement reached by two or more people to carry out an action. It means *to agree to do something*:

Quedamos en salir todos *We arranged to all go out*
juntos esta noche. *together tonight.*

■ **38.1.7** **Dejar de** + the infinitive and **parar de** + the infinitive indicate that a habitual action in the past has now ceased or will do so:

Ha dejado de fumar. *I've given up smoking.*
Para de beber, por favor. *Stop drinking please.*

■ **38.1.8** **Llegar a** + the infinitive indicates the consequence of an action:

Se enfadaron tanto que *They got so angry that they*
hasta **llegaron a** *even ended by insulting each*
insultarse. *other.*

■ **38.1.9** Phrasal verbs + the infinitive expressing obligation:

a **Tener que** + the infinitive and **haber que** + the infinitive express obligation or necessity:

Tengo que escribir una *I have to write a letter.*
carta.

b **Haber que** is only used in the third person as the impersonal form **hay que**:

Hay que trabajar más. *One must work harder.*

Haber de + the infinitive:
He de tomar el avión de   *I have to catch the five o'clock*
las cinco.   *plane.*

c **Deber** + the infinitive:
Debes reservar una   *You should reserve a room soon.*
habitación pronto.

Note the difference with **deber de** + the infinitive, which expresses probability or supposition:
Debe de tener unos   *He must be about fifty.*
cincuenta años.

38.2 Phrasal Verbs with the Gerund

■ **38.2.1** **Estar** + gerund expresses the present progressive (see 23.4):

Está comiendo.   *He is eating.*

■ **38.2.2** **Seguir/continuar** + gerund expresses continuity in an action:

Sigue estudiando español   *He continues to study Spanish*
aunque lo habla muy bien.   *although he speaks it very well.*

■ **38.2.3** **Llevar** + the gerund expresses a temporary action that starts in the past and continues in the present. It is the equivalent of the construction **hace . . . que**:

Llevo dos años   *I've been living in Tijuana*
viviendo en Tijuana.   *for two years.*
(= Hace dos años que
vivo en Tijuana.)

■ **38.2.4** **Quedarse** + gerund expresses duration and continuity of an action:

Se quedó viendo la   *He stayed up watching television*
televisión hasta muy tarde.   *until very late.*

38.3 Phrasal Verbs with Participles

Some verbs such as **llevar**, **tener**, **estar**, and **ser**, and sometimes **traer**, **quedar**, and **dejar**, can be followed by a participle. In these cases, the participle changes in gender and in number:

El coche **lleva recorridos**   *The car has done 400*
400 kilómetros.   *kilometers (250 miles).*

Tengo pensado ir de   *I've decided to go to Venezuela*
vacaciones a Venezuela.   *for my vacation.*

Dejó dicho que lo   *He told them to call him in the*
llamaran por la mañana.   *morning.*

For constructions with **ser** see section 34.

39 Modal Verbs

Spanish has a smaller number of modal verbs than English. They indicate the attitude of the subject toward an action expressed by an infinitive. Their main function is to express intentions or opinions, and they are followed by an infinitive. Usually the infinitive and the main verb share the same subject. In Spanish modal verbs can be used in all tenses.

39.1 Common Modal Verbs

deber	*should, ought to, must*
poder	*can, could, may, might, be able*
querer	*want, will, would like*
saber	*know, know how to, be able*
soler	*usually, be used to*

Debe trabajar.	*He should/ought to work.*
Puede trabajar.	*He can work.*
Quiere trabajar.	*He wants to work.*
Sabe trabajar.	*He knows how to work.*
Suele trabajar.	*He usually works.*

39.2 *Saber* and *Poder*

■ **39.2.1** In Spanish the ability to do something is expressed by **saber**. **Saber** in this case means *can do something*:

Sé tocar el piano.	*I can play the piano.*
El niño **no sabe nadar**.	*The child cannot swim.*

■ **39.2.2** **Poder** is only used in this context to express a physical ability:

Puedo correr diez kilómetros sin cansarme.	*I can run ten kilometers (6 miles) without getting tired.*

40 *Ser* and *Estar*

Ser and **estar** are two verbs that correspond in English to one verb, *to be*.

40.1 Use of *Ser*

■ **40.1.1** Grammatically **ser** is always used before a noun, a noun phrase, a pronoun, a determiner (numerals, demonstratives, indefinites), and infinitives:

Es María.	*It's María.*
Es mío.	*It's mine.*
Soy yo.	*It's me.*
En mi familia **somos** cinco chicos y dos chicas.	*There are five boys and two girls in our family.*
Esto **es** vivir.	*This is living.*
No **es** esta calle, **es** otra.	*It's not this street; it's another one.*

For the conjugation of **ser** and **estar** see section 42.

Ser is used in the following cases:

a To express identity or to identify someone or something:

Soy María Martínez.	*I am María Martínez.*
Es un libro de español.	*It's a Spanish book.*

b To express profession:

Soy médico.	*I'm a doctor.*

See section 6.2.4 for use of **ser** with professions.

c To describe a relationship:

Es mi padre.	*He's my father.*

d With nationality, origin, or religious, political, or artistic affiliation:

Soy española.	*I'm Spanish.*
Soy andaluz.	*I'm Andalusian.*

Es musulmán.	*He's a Muslim.*
El cuadro **es** surrealista.	*The painting is surrealist.*

e To say what something is made of:

Es de plástico.	*It's made of plastic.*

f To express possession:

Esta cartera **es** mía.	*This briefcase is mine.*

See possessive adjectives and pronouns in section 12.

g Time and dates:

Son las dos.	*It's two o'clock.*
Es martes.	*It's Tuesday.*
Es uno de enero.	*It's the first of January.*

h Price, number, quantity, and order:

Son dos mil pesos.	*They cost two thousand pesos.*
Mi número favorito **es** el cinco.	*My favorite number is five.*
Es poco dinero.	*It's not much money.*
Es el primero de la clase.	*He's at the top of the class.*

i In impersonal expressions such as:

Es interesante.	*It's interesting.*
Es importante.	*It's important.*
Es malo.	*It's bad.*

j To express location of events with the meaning *to take place*:

La fiesta **es** en casa de Marta.	*The party is in Marta's house.*

40.2 Use of *Estar*

a **Estar** is used to express location. It answers the question ¿**dónde está**? (*where is it?*):

Bogotá **está** en el centro de Colombia.	*Bogota is in the center of Colombia.*

b It is also used with dates:

¿A qué día **estamos**?　　*What's the date today?*
Estamos a ocho de mayo.　*It's the eighth of May.*

c **Estar** followed by **de** is used to express temporary situations:

Está de recepcionista　　*She's working as a receptionist*
este verano.　　　　　　*this summer.*
El color rojo **está de**　　*The color red is*
moda.　　　　　　　　　*fashionable.*

d Used with **con** (*with*) it can also express temporary situations:

Está con un fuerte resfriado. *He has a bad cold.*

e Used with the adverbs **bien**, **mal**, and **regular** (*not bad, so-so*) it expresses physical and mental state:

¿Qué tal **estás**?　　　*How are you?*
Estoy bien, gracias.　　*I'm well, thanks.*

f Used with a personal pronoun it means *it suits* or *fits me/you/her*, etc:

La falda **te está** muy bien.　*The skirt suits you very well.*

g **Estar** followed by **por** or **para** means that something is on the point of being done or needs to be done, or that someone is on the point of doing something:

La limpieza aún **está por**　*The cleaning is still to be done.*
hacer.
El premio **está por** salir.　*The prize is about to be*
　　　　　　　　　　　　announced.
La obra **está para** empezar. *The play is going to start.*

40.3 Use with Adjectives of Quality

The use of **ser** and **estar** with adjectives of quality depends not on the quality itself, but on the way the speaker perceives that quality.

■ 40.3.1 Ser + adjective is used to express:

• an inherent quality

• a sense of permanency

• integrated features

It is often related to personality or character, colors, or shapes—something that cannot change or has not changed:

Es inteligente.	*She's intelligent.*
Es simpático.	*He's nice.*
Es redondo.	*It's round.*
Es verde.	*It's green.*

■ 40.3.2 Estar + adjective expresses:

• a more subjective quality

• a physical or psychological state that might change or is the result of a change.

La botella **está** vacía.	*The bottle is empty.*
La puerta **está** cerrada.	*The door is closed.*
Luis **está** contento.	*Luis is happy.*
La casa **está** sucia.	*The house is dirty.*

Note that the adjectives **roto** (*broken*) and **muerto** (*dead*), despite implying permanence, are used with **estar** because they are the result of change.

El vaso **está** roto.	*The glass is broken.*
El perro **está** muerto.	*The dog is dead.*

■ 40.3.3 Note the differences in the following expressions:

Está casado. (adjective)	*He's married.*
Es casado. (noun)	*He's a married man.*
Está soltero. (adjective)	*He's single.*
Es soltero. (noun)	*He's a single man.*

Está divorciada. (adjective)	*She's divorced.*
Es divorciada. (noun)	*She's a divorcee.*
Está viuda. (adjective)	*She's widowed.*
Es viuda. (noun)	*She's a widow.*

For past participles used adjectivally see section 30.3.

40.4 *Ser* and *Estar* in Contrast

Ser and **estar** can be used with the same adjectives, but give different meanings.
The choice of one or the other with the same adjective depends on the decision of the speaker in terms of his or her perception of the situation:

Juan **es** tranquilo.	*Juan is quiet (a quiet man).*
Juan **está** tranquilo.	*Juan is relaxed.*

The first sentence refers to Juan's personality—*Juan is a quiet person*; the second refers to a temporary state—*Juan is relaxed* (today because he has finished his exams).

■ **40.4.1 Ser** is used in more general, objective statements while **estar** is used in subjective statements.

■ **40.4.2** When a quality is perceived as being a real or possible change, depending on different circumstances, **estar** is used. In these cases **estar** can often be substituted by verbs meaning *to feel* or *to look*:

El niño **está** muy alto. Ha crecido mucho desde que lo vi.	*The boy is very tall. He's grown a lot since I last saw him.*
La señora Pérez **está** muy joven para su edad; ya tiene 70 años.	*Mrs. Pérez looks very young for her age; she's seventy years old.*
La casa **está** muy bonita para la fiesta de mañana.	*The house is looking very pretty for tomorrow's party.*

Estoy muy nervioso porque tengo un examen.	*I'm very nervous because I've got an exam.*
Está muy gordo. Ha engordado 20 kilos en un año.	*He's very fat. He's put on 20 kilos (45 pounds) in a year.*

■ **40.4.3** If **ser** is used instead of **estar** in the above sentences, the meaning is quite different and the quality expressed is perceived as permanent, independent of any circumstance:

El niño **es** muy alto. Es el más alto de sus amigos.	*The boy is very tall. He's the tallest of his friends.*
La señora Pérez **es** joven; tiene 23 años.	*Mrs. Pérez is young; she's twenty-three years old.*
Esta casa **es** muy bonita, **es** mucho mejor que la mía.	*This house is very pretty; it's much better than mine.*
Soy muy nervioso. **Es** mi carácter.	*I am very nervous. It's my character.*
Juan **es** gordo. Yo siempre lo he conocido así.	*Juan is fat. I have always known him that way.*

Other useful examples are:

El cielo **es** azul.	*The sky is blue.*
El cielo **está** azul hoy.	*The sky is blue today.*
El café **es** amargo.	*Coffee is bitter.*
El café **está** amargo; no tiene azúcar.	*The coffee is bitter; it has no sugar.*
La fruta **es** cara.	*Fruit is expensive.*
La fruta **está** cara en invierno.	*Fruit is expensive in winter.*
La paella **es** buena.	*Paella is good.*
La paella **está** buena en este restaurante.	*The paella is good in this restaurant.*

| La casa **es** fría. | *The house is cold.* |
| La casa **está** fría; no hay calefacción. | *The house is cold; it has no heating.* |

■ **40.4.4** Some adjectives change meaning when used with either **ser** or **estar**:

| Luis **es** muy malo. (de carácter) | *Luis is very bad.* *(character)* |
| Luis **está** malo. (de salud) | *Luis is ill. (health)* |

| María **es** lista. | *María is clever.* |
| María **está** lista. | *María is ready.* |

| Juan **es** aburrido. | *Juan is boring.* |
| Juan **está** aburrido. | *Juan is bored.* |

| El niño **es** vivo. | *The child is quick-witted.* |
| El niño **está** vivo. | *The child is alive.* |

40.5 Use in Passive Constructions

■ **40.5.1** Both **ser** and **estar** are used in passive constructions. **Ser** is the verb used in most cases:

| La casa **es** construída por el ayuntamiento. (Está a medio construir, no está terminada.) | *The house is being built by the council. (It's half-built; it isn't finished.)* |

■ **40.5.2** The passive with **ser** expresses the action in the process of being done, while with **estar** it is the end or result of the action that is being stressed:

| La casa **está** construída. (**Está** terminada.) | *The house is built. (It is finished.)* |

For use of **ser** in passive constructions see section 34. For use of **estar** with gerunds (*-ing* forms) see 23.4.

41 Regular Verbs

41.1 Conjugation of Verbs Ending in -ar

Example: hablar (*to speak*)

	PERSON	PRESENT	IMPERFECT	PRETERITE
	1st	habl-o	habl-aba	habl-é
sing	2nd	-as	-abas	-aste
	3rd	-a	-aba	-ó
	1st	-amos	-ábamos	-amos
plur	2nd	-áis	-abais	-asteis
	3rd	-an	-aban	-aron

	PERSON	FUTURE	CONDITIONAL
	1st	hablar-é	hablar-ía
sing	2nd	-ás	-ías
	3rd	-á	-ía
	1st	-emos	-íamos
plur	2nd	-éis	-íais
	3rd	-án	-ían

	PERSON	PRESENT SUBJUNCTIVE	IMPERFECT SUBJUNCTIVE
	1st	habl-e	habl-ara/-ase
sing	2nd	-es	-aras/-ases
	3rd	-e	-ara/-ase
	1st	-emos	-áramos/-ásemos
plur	2nd	-éis	-arais/-aseis
	3rd	-en	-aran/-asen

PAST PARTICIPLE: habl-ado

GERUND: habl-ando

IMPERATIVE: (tú) habl-a, (vosotros) habl-ad

41.2 Conjugation of Verbs Ending in *-er*

Example: com**er** (*to eat*)

	PERSON	PRESENT	IMPERFECT	PRETERITE
	1st	com-**o**	com-**ía**	com-**í**
sing	2nd	-**es**	-**ías**	-**iste**
	3rd	-**e**	-**ía**	-**ió**
	1st	-**emos**	-**íamos**	-**imos**
plur	2nd	-**éis**	-**íais**	-**isteis**
	3rd	-**en**	-**ían**	-**ieron**

	PERSON	FUTURE	CONDITIONAL
	1st	comer-**é**	comer-**ía**
sing	2nd	-**ás**	-**ías**
	3rd	-**á**	-**ía**
	1st	-**emos**	-**íamos**
plur	2nd	-**éis**	-**íais**
	3rd	-**án**	-**ían**

	PERSON	PRESENT SUBJUNCTIVE	IMPERFECT SUBJUNCTIVE
	1st	com-**a**	com-**iera/-iese**
sing	2nd	-**as**	-**ieras/-ieses**
	3rd	-**a**	-**iera/-iese**
	1st	-**amos**	-**iéramos/-iésemos**
plur	2nd	-**áis**	-**ierais/-ieseis**
	3rd	-**an**	-**ieran/iesen**

PAST PARTICIPLE: com-**ido**

GERUND: com-**iendo**

IMPERATIVE: (**tú**) com-**e**, (**vosotros**) com-**ed**

41.3 Conjugation of Verbs Ending in -ir

Example: viv**ir** (*to live*)

	PERSON	PRESENT	IMPERFECT	PRETERITE
	1st	viv-**o**	viv-**ía**	viv-**í**
sing	2nd	-es	-ías	-iste
	3rd	-e	-ía	-ió
	1st	-imos	-íamos	-imos
plur	2nd	-ís	-íais	-isteis
	3rd	-en	-ían	-ieron

	PERSON	FUTURE	CONDITIONAL
	1st	vivir-**é**	vivir-**ía**
sing	2nd	-ás	-ías
	3rd	-á	-ía
	1st	-emos	-íamos
plur	2nd	-éis	-íais
	3rd	-án	-ían

	PERSON	PRESENT SUBJUNCTIVE	IMPERFECT SUBJUNCTIVE
	1st	viv-**a**	viv-**iera/-iese**
sing	2nd	-as	-ieras/-ieses
	3rd	-a	-iera/-iese
	1st	-amos	-iéramos/-iésemos
plur	2nd	-áis	-ierais/-ieseis
	3rd	-an	-ieran/-iesen

PAST PARTICIPLE: viv-**ido**

GERUND: viv-**iendo**

IMPERATIVE: (**tú**) viv-**e**, (**vosotros**) viv-**id**

41.4 Compound Tenses

They are formed with the past participle of the verb
preceded by the auxiliary verb **haber**, conjugated.
The past participle is formed from the infinitive, dropping
the infinitive endings and adding the past participle
endings **-ado**, **-ido**, **-ido**:

Ha lle**gado** tarde.   *He has arrived late.*

• The present perfect tense is formed with the present
  tense of **haber** plus the past participle:

		comprar	**comer**	**vivir**
		-ado	**-ido**	**-ido**
	1st	he comp**rado**	com**ido**	viv**ido**
sing	2nd	has		
	3rd	ha		
	1st	hemos		
plur	2nd	habéis		
	3rd	han		

• The pluperfect, or past perfect, is formed with the
  imperfect tense of **haber** plus the past participle:

	1st	había comp**rado**	com**ido**	viv**ido**
sing	2nd	habías		
	3rd	había		
	1st	habíamos		
plur	2nd	habíais		
	3rd	habían		

• The future perfect is formed with the future tense of
  haber plus the past participle:

	1st	habré comp**rado**	com**ido**	viv**ido**
sing	2nd	habrás		
	3rd	habrá		
	1st	habremos		
plur	2nd	habréis		
	3rd	habrán		

- The conditional perfect is formed with the conditional tense of **haber** plus the past participle:

	1st	habría compr**ado**	com**ido**	viv**ido**
sing	2nd	habrías		
	3rd	habría		
	1st	habríamos		
plur	2nd	habríais		
	3rd	habrían		

- The preterite perfect is formed with the preterite of **haber** plus the past participle:

	1st	hube compr**ado**	com**ido**	viv**ido**
sing	2nd	hubiste		
	3rd	hubo		
	1st	hubimos		
plur	2nd	hubisteis		
	3rd	hubieron		

- The present perfect subjunctive is formed with the present subjunctive of **haber** plus the past participle:

	1st	haya compr**ado**	com**ido**	viv**ido**
sing	2nd	hayas		
	3rd	haya		
	1st	hayamos		
plur	2nd	hayáis		
	3rd	hayan		

- The past perfect subjunctive is formed with the imperfect subjunctive of **haber** plus the past participle:

	1st	hubiera/hubiese compr**ado**	com**ido**	viv**ido**
sing	2nd	hubieras/hubieses		
	3rd	hubiera/hubiese		
	1st	hubiéramos/hubiésemos		
plur	2nd	hubierais/hubieseis		
	3rd	hubieran/hubiesen		

For irregular verbs see section 42.

42.1 Dar (*to give*)

	PERSON	PRESENT	IMPERFECT	PRETERITE
	1st	doy	daba	di
sing	2nd	das	dabas	diste
	3rd	da	daba	dio
	1st	damos	dábamos	dimos
plur	2nd	dais	dabais	disteis
	3rd	dan	daban	dieron

	PERSON	FUTURE	CONDITIONAL
	1st	daré	daría
sing	2nd	darás	darías
	3rd	dará	daría
	1st	daremos	daríamos
plur	2nd	daréis	daríais
	3rd	darán	darían

	PERSON	PRESENT SUBJUNCTIVE	IMPERFECT SUBJUNCTIVE
	1st	dé	diera/diese
sing	2nd	des	dieras/dieses
	3rd	dé	diera/diese
	1st	demos	diéramos/diésemos
plur	2nd	deis	dierais/dieseis
	3rd	den	dieran/diesen

PAST PARTICIPLE: dado

GERUND: dando

IMPERATIVE: (tú) da, (vosotros) dad

42.2 Decir (*to say/tell*)

	PERSON	PRESENT	IMPERFECT	PRETERITE
	1st	digo	decía	dije
sing	2nd	dices	decías	dijiste
	3rd	dice	decía	dijo
	1st	decimos	decíamos	dijimos
plur	2nd	decís	decíais	dijisteis
	3rd	dicen	decían	dijeron

		FUTURE	CONDITIONAL
	1st	diré	diría
sing	2nd	dirás	dirías
	3rd	dirá	diría
	1st	diremos	diríamos
plur	2nd	diréis	diríais
	3rd	dirán	dirían

		PRESENT SUBJUNCTIVE	IMPERFECT SUBJUNCTIVE
	1st	diga	dijera/dijese
sing	2nd	digas	dijeras/dijeses
	3rd	diga	dijera/dijese
	1st	digamos	dijéramos/dijésemos
plur	2nd	digáis	dijerais/dijeseis
	3rd	digan	dijeran/dijesen

PAST PARTICIPLE: dicho

GERUND: diciendo

IMPERATIVE: (tú) di, (vosotros) decid

42.3 Estar (*to be*)

	PERSON	PRESENT	IMPERFECT	PRETERITE
	1st	estoy	estaba	estuve
sing	2nd	estás	estabas	estuviste
	3rd	está	estaba	estuvo
	1st	estamos	estábamos	estuvimos
plur	2nd	estáis	estabais	estuvisteis
	3rd	están	estaban	estuvieron

		FUTURE	CONDITIONAL
	1st	estaré	estaría
sing	2nd	estarás	estarías
	3rd	estará	estaría
	1st	estaremos	estaríamos
plur	2nd	estaréis	estaríais
	3rd	estarán	estarían

		PRESENT SUBJUNCTIVE	IMPERFECT SUBJUNCTIVE
	1st	esté	estuviera/estuviese
sing	2nd	estés	estuvieras/estuvieses
	3rd	esté	estuviera/estuviese
	1st	estemos	estuviéramos/estuviésemos
plur	2nd	estéis	estuvierais/estuvieseis
	3rd	estén	estuvieran/estuviesen

PAST PARTICIPLE: estado

GERUND: estando

IMPERATIVE: (tú) está(te), (vosotros) estad

42.4 Haber* (*to have*)

	PERSON	PRESENT	IMPERFECT	PRETERITE
	1st	he	había	hube
sing	2nd	has	habías	hubiste
	3rd	ha	había	hubo
	1st	hemos	habíamos	hubimos
plur	2nd	habéis	habíais	hubisteis
	3rd	han	habían	hubieron

		FUTURE	CONDITIONAL
	1st	habré	habría
sing	2nd	habrás	habrías
	3rd	habrá	habría
	1st	habremos	habríamos
plur	2nd	habréis	habríais
	3rd	habrán	habrían

		PRESENT SUBJUNCTIVE	IMPERFECT SUBJUNCTIVE
	1st	haya	hubiera/hubiese
sing	2nd	hayas	hubieras/hubieses
	3rd	haya	hubiera/hubiese
	1st	hayamos	hubiéramos/hubiésemos
plur	2nd	hayáis	hubierais/hubieseis
	3rd	hayan	hubieran/hubiesen

PAST PARTICIPLE: habido

GERUND: habiendo

*mainly used as an auxiliary verb

42.5 Hacer (*to do/make*)

	PERSON	PRESENT	IMPERFECT	PRETERITE
	1st	hago	hacía	hice
sing	2nd	haces	hacías	hiciste
	3rd	hace	hacía	hizo
	1st	hacemos	hacíamos	hicimos
plur	2nd	hacéis	hacíais	hicisteis
	3rd	hacen	hacían	hicieron

		FUTURE	CONDITIONAL
	1st	haré	haría
sing	2nd	harás	harías
	3rd	hará	haría
	1st	haremos	haríamos
plur	2nd	haréis	haríais
	3rd	harán	harían

		PRESENT SUBJUNCTIVE	IMPERFECT SUBJUNCTIVE
	1st	haga	hiciera/hiciese
sing	2nd	hagas	hicieras/hicieses
	3rd	haga	hiciera/hiciese
	1st	hagamos	hiciéramos/hiciésemos
plur	2nd	hagáis	hicierais/hicieseis
	3rd	hagan	hicieran/hiciesen

PAST PARTICIPLE: hecho

GERUND: haciendo

IMPERATIVE: (tú) haz, (vosotros) haced

42.6 Ir (*to go*)

	PERSON	PRESENT	IMPERFECT	PRETERITE
	1st	voy	iba	fui
sing	2nd	vas	ibas	fuiste
	3rd	va	iba	fue
	1st	vamos	íbamos	fuimos
plur	2nd	vais	ibais	fuisteis
	3rd	van	iban	fueron

	PERSON	FUTURE	CONDITIONAL
	1st	iré	iría
sing	2nd	irás	irías
	3rd	irá	iría
	1st	iremos	iríamos
plur	2nd	iréis	iríais
	3rd	irán	irían

	PERSON	PRESENT SUBJUNCTIVE	IMPERFECT SUBJUNCTIVE
	1st	vaya	fuera/fuese
sing	2nd	vayas	fueras/fueses
	3rd	vaya	fuera/fuese
	1st	vayamos	fuéramos/fuésemos
plur	2nd	vayáis	fuerais/fueseis
	3rd	vayan	fueran/fuesen

PAST PARTICIPLE: ido

GERUND: yendo

IMPERATIVE: (tú) ve, (vosotros) id

42.7 Poder (*to be able*)

	PERSON	PRESENT	IMPERFECT	PRETERITE
	1st	puedo	podía	pude
sing	2nd	puedes	podías	pudiste
	3rd	puede	podía	pudo
	1st	podemos	podíamos	pudimos
plur	2nd	podéis	podíais	pudisteis
	3rd	pueden	podían	pudieron

		FUTURE	CONDITIONAL
	1st	podré	podría
sing	2nd	podrás	podrías
	3rd	podrá	podría
	1st	podremos	podríamos
plur	2nd	podréis	podríais
	3rd	podrán	podrían

		PRESENT SUBJUNCTIVE	IMPERFECT SUBJUNCTIVE
	1st	pueda	pudiera/pudiese
sing	2nd	puedas	pudieras/pudieses
	3rd	pueda	pudiera/pudiese
	1st	podamos	pudiéramos/pudiésemos
plur	2nd	podáis	pudierais/pudieseis
	3rd	puedan	pudieran/pudiesen

PAST PARTICIPLE: podido

GERUND: pudiendo

42.8 Poner (*to put*)

	PERSON	PRESENT	IMPERFECT	PRETERITE
	1st	pongo	ponía	puse
sing	2nd	pones	ponías	pusiste
	3rd	pone	ponía	puso
	1st	ponemos	poníamos	pusimos
plur	2nd	ponéis	poníais	pusisteis
	3rd	ponen	ponían	pusieron

		FUTURE	CONDITIONAL
	1st	pondré	pondría
sing	2nd	pondrás	pondrías
	3rd	pondrá	pondría
	1st	pondremos	pondríamos
plur	2nd	pondréis	pondríais
	3rd	pondrán	pondrían

		PRESENT SUBJUNCTIVE	IMPERFECT SUBJUNCTIVE
	1st	ponga	pusiera/pusiese
sing	2nd	pongas	pusieras/pusieses
	3rd	ponga	pusiera/pusiese
	1st	pongamos	pusiéramos/pusiésemos
plur	2nd	pongáis	pusierais/pusieseis
	3rd	pongan	pusieran/pusiesen

PAST PARTICIPLE: puesto

GERUND: poniendo

IMPERATIVE: (tú) pon, (vosotros) poned

42.9 Querer (*to want*)

	PERSON	PRESENT	IMPERFECT	PRETERITE
	1st	quiero	quería	quise
sing	2nd	quieres	querías	quisiste
	3rd	quiere	quería	quiso
	1st	queremos	queríamos	quisimos
plur	2nd	queréis	queríais	quisisteis
	3rd	quieren	querían	quisieron

		FUTURE	CONDITIONAL
	1st	querré	querría
sing	2nd	querrás	querrías
	3rd	querrá	querría
	1st	querremos	querríamos
plur	2nd	querréis	querríais
	3rd	querrán	querrían

		PRESENT SUBJUNCTIVE	IMPERFECT SUBJUNCTIVE
	1st	quiera	quisiera/quisiese
sing	2nd	quieras	quisieras/quisieses
	3rd	quiera	quisiera/quisiese
	1st	queramos	quisiéramos/quisiésemos
plur	2nd	queráis	quisierais/quisieseis
	3rd	quieran	quisieran/quisiesen

PAST PARTICIPLE: querido

GERUND: queriendo

IMPERATIVE: (tú) quiere, (vosotros) quered

42.10 Saber (*to know*)

	PERSON	PRESENT	IMPERFECT	PRETERITE
	1st	sé	sabía	supe
sing	2nd	sabes	sabías	supiste
	3rd	sabe	sabía	supo
	1st	sabemos	sabíamos	supimos
plur	2nd	sabéis	sabíais	supisteis
	3rd	saben	sabían	supieron

		FUTURE	CONDITIONAL
	1st	sabré	sabría
sing	2nd	sabrás	sabrías
	3rd	sabrá	sabría
	1st	sabremos	sabríamos
plur	2nd	sabréis	sabríais
	3rd	sabrán	sabrían

		PRESENT SUBJUNCTIVE	IMPERFECT SUBJUNCTIVE
	1st	sepa	supiera/supiese
sing	2nd	sepas	supieras/supieses
	3rd	sepa	supiera/supiese
	1st	sepamos	supiéramos/supiésemos
plur	2nd	sepáis	supierais/supieseis
	3rd	sepan	supieran/supiesen

PAST PARTICIPLE: sabido

GERUND: sabiendo

IMPERATIVE: (tú) sabe, (vosotros) sabed

42.11 Ser (*to be*)

	PERSON	PRESENT	IMPERFECT	PRETERITE
	1st	soy	era	fui
sing	2nd	eres	eras	fuiste
	3rd	es	era	fue
	1st	somos	éramos	fuimos
plur	2nd	sois	erais	fuisteis
	3rd	son	eran	fueron

		FUTURE	CONDITIONAL
	1st	seré	sería
sing	2nd	serás	serías
	3rd	será	sería
	1st	seremos	seríamos
plur	2nd	seréis	seríais
	3rd	serán	serían

		PRESENT SUBJUNCTIVE	IMPERFECT SUBJUNCTIVE
	1st	sea	fuera/fuese
sing	2nd	seas	fueras/fueses
	3rd	sea	fuera/fuese
	1st	seamos	fuéramos/fuésemos
plur	2nd	seáis	fuerais/fueseis
	3rd	sean	fueran/fuesen

PAST PARTICIPLE: sido

GERUND: siendo

IMPERATIVE: (tú) sé, (vosotros) sed

42.12 Tener (*to have*)

	PERSON	PRESENT	IMPERFECT	PRETERITE
	1st	tengo	tenía	tuve
sing	2nd	tienes	tenías	tuviste
	3rd	tiene	tenía	tuvo
	1st	tenemos	teníamos	tuvimos
plur	2nd	tenéis	teníais	tuvisteis
	3rd	tienen	tenían	tuvieron

		FUTURE	CONDITIONAL
	1st	tendré	tendría
sing	2nd	tendrás	tendrías
	3rd	tendrá	tendría
	1st	tendremos	tendríamos
plur	2nd	tendréis	tendríais
	3rd	tendrán	tendrían

		PRESENT SUBJUNCTIVE	IMPERFECT SUBJUNCTIVE
	1st	tenga	tuviera/tuviese
sing	2nd	tengas	tuvieras/tuvieses
	3rd	tenga	tuviera/tuviese
	1st	tengamos	tuviéramos/tuviésemos
plur	2nd	tengáis	tuvierais/tuvieseis
	3rd	tengan	tuvieran/tuviesen

PAST PARTICIPLE: tenido

GERUND: teniendo

IMPERATIVE: (tú) ten, (vosotros) tened

42.13 Traer (*to bring*)

	PERSON	PRESENT	IMPERFECT	PRETERITE
	1st	traigo	traía	traje
sing	2nd	traes	traías	trajiste
	3rd	trae	traía	trajo
	1st	traemos	traíamos	trajimos
plur	2nd	traéis	traíais	trajisteis
	3rd	traen	traían	trajeron

		FUTURE	CONDITIONAL
	1st	traeré	traería
sing	2nd	traerás	traerías
	3rd	traerá	traería
	1st	traeremos	traeríamos
plur	2nd	traeréis	traeríais
	3rd	traerán	traerían

		PRESENT SUBJUNCTIVE	IMPERFECT SUBJUNCTIVE
	1st	traiga	trajera/trajese
sing	2nd	traigas	trajeras/trajeses
	3rd	traiga	trajera/trajese
	1st	traigamos	trajéramos/trajésemos
plur	2nd	traigáis	trajerais/trajeseis
	3rd	traigan	trajeran/trajesen

PAST PARTICIPLE: traído

GERUND: trayendo

IMPERATIVE: (tú) trae, (vosotros) traed

42.14 Venir (*to come*)

	PERSON	PRESENT	IMPERFECT	PRETERITE
	1st	vengo	venía	vine
sing	2nd	vienes	venías	viniste
	3rd	viene	venía	vino
	1st	venimos	veníamos	vinimos
plur	2nd	venís	veníais	vinisteis
	3rd	vienen	venían	vinieron

		FUTURE	CONDITIONAL
	1st	vendré	vendría
sing	2nd	vendrás	vendrías
	3rd	vendrá	vendría
	1st	vendremos	vendríamos
plur	2nd	vendréis	vendríais
	3rd	vendrán	vendrían

		PRESENT SUBJUNCTIVE	IMPERFECT SUBJUNCTIVE
	1st	venga	viniera/viniese
sing	2nd	vengas	vinieras/vinieses
	3rd	venga	viniera/viniese
	1st	vengamos	viniéramos/viniésemos
plur	2nd	vengáis	vinierais/vinieseis
	3rd	vengan	vinieran/viniesen

PAST PARTICIPLE: venido

GERUND: viniendo

IMPERATIVE: (tú) ven, (vosotros) venid

42.15 Irregularities in Other Verbs

Verbs that present irregularities in only some of their tenses:

abrir　　past participle: **abierto**

andar　　preterite: **anduve, anduviste, anduvo**, etc.
　　　　　　imperfect subjunctive: **anduviera/anduviese**, etc.

conducir　present: **conduzco, conduces**, etc.
　　　　　　preterite: **conduje, condujiste**, etc.

cubrir　　past participle: **cubierto**

escribir　past participle: **escrito**

morir　　past participle: **muerto**

oír　　　present: **oigo, oyes**, etc.

romper　past participle: **roto**

salir　　present: **salgo, sales**, etc.

soltar　　past participle: **suelto**

ver　　　past participle: **visto**

volver　　past participle: **vuelto**

There are more irregular verbs in Spanish, but section 42 has covered the most common ones.

■ Index

This index lists key words in Spanish and English as well as grammatical terms. Many references are included under several different headings. For example, if you want to find out how to say *you* in Spanish, you can look up any of the following entries: *you*, **tú** or **usted**, "subject pronouns," or "personal pronouns."